Assessment and Accountability in Language Education Programs

A Guide for Administrators and Teachers

Margo Gottlieb

Diep Nguyen

Caslon Publishing
Philadelphia

Dedication
To B.J.S.
and language learners everywhere

Caslon Publishing
P.O. Box 3248
Philadelphia, PA 19130

www.caslonpublishing.com

9 8 7 6 5 4 3 2 1

Library of Congress Cataloging-in-Publication Data

Gottleib, Margo H.
    Assessment and accountability in language education programs : a guide for
administrators and teachers / Margo Gottlieb, Diep Nguyen.
        p.   cm.
    Includes bibliographical references and index.
    ISBN 0-9727507-7-0 (pbk. : alk. paper)
 1. English language—Study and teaching—Foreign speakers.   2. English
language—Ability testing.
 I. Nguyen, Diep, 1958–   II. Title.
    PE1128 .A2G658 2007
      428 ' .0071—dc22   2006100728

Foreword

This wonderful book could not have appeared at a better time. We are most fortunate that Margo Gottlieb and Diep Nguyen have created a rational and durable framework for orchestrating the competing demands on educators for accountability, program improvement, and appropriate classroom instruction. They delineate the complex issues of assessment in linguistically diverse settings and address the different dimensions along which educators are asked to evaluate their students and their programs. More important, they provide a blueprint for the creation of a comprehensive assessment system, gained through the application of their ideas in practice. Their work is predicated on the premise that assessment is conducted at different levels for different purposes, all of which are valid. There is not a hierarchy in which some are the real or most important assessments, but rather the different dimensions function in a dynamic relationship that is constantly evolving.

Those of us who have dedicated our careers to working with second-language learners are used to having our specific concerns dealt with perfunctorily as an afterthought in reform efforts. This book does the opposite. It puts the needs of linguistically diverse students at the center of the planning process, and in so doing takes into account the needs of all students. The narrative provides a detailed history of how the framework has been implemented in an elementary school district in Schaumburg, Illinois. School District 54 has a diverse student population—something increasingly encountered in all school districts—and employs a variety of program types to meet the needs of its second-language learners. The account of SD 54's efforts to create an assessment system that meets the needs of its linguistically diverse population helps all language teachers gain the confidence we need to critically analyze and improve our work. The combination of theory, example, and working documents provides the necessary tools to build a comprehensive assessment plan that is flexible enough to be adapted to virtually any kind of programming for linguistically and culturally diverse student populations. We are lucky indeed that the leadership of SD 54 had the wisdom and political will to undertake this important work and share the process and the results with us.

In the course of writing this book, the authors continually refined their thinking to make their ideas accessible and applicable to real-life classrooms in the context of a shifting political landscape. As a result, they do not advocate a particular program type or mode of delivery, nor do they set out a list of "must-do" assessments. Rather, they provide an overview of the types of information needed to answer critical questions at the state, district, program, and classroom level. The BASIC model proposed in this book allows assessment and accountability procedures to be fine-tuned as external mandates change and programmatic demands are adjusted.

Currently, out of necessity, educational improvement efforts are focused on narrowly defined measures used for program accountability. Despite the very real need to meet external accountability requirements, the authors never lose sight of the foundational concerns that drive evaluation: What do we want students to know and be able to do, and how will we know we have accomplished our goals? Teachers need to document exactly where their students begin, how they have progressed, and where they need to go next in their academic development. Program developers need to determine if what they are doing works, and schools and districts need to assure the community that all students are provided with the means to achieve to their maximum potential.

Every school district in the country can benefit from this book, no matter what their demographic profile. The ideas will help all educators approach the complex task of assessment and accountability with confidence. To say that this book is valuable for all teachers does not diminish its particular importance for educators of English language learners. The BASIC model described in this book allows for an in-depth analysis of language education programs and addresses the fundamental challenge to educators of ELLs, that of distinguishing academic achievement from language development. The myriad challenges educators face in designing programs to meet the needs of an extremely varied student population are taken up in this book, and solutions are offered. The authors recognize that we must strive to meet educational benchmarks while at the same time providing the kind of instruction that will help students succeed and progress in language learning. A key to the strength of the BASIC model described in this book is that it can be used to document both the attainment of benchmarks and the actual progress that students make in learning.

Evaluation, as the authors point out, has its highest utility when reflected back into the learning environment itself. With the tools of the BASIC model in hand, teachers in different types of language programs can use the results of evaluations to make instructional decisions. An important contribution of the book and the BASIC model is to show how information from a variety of sources can be aggregated and evaluated in assisting the language learning of students whose first language is not English. The authors suggest how to include learning and instruction in two languages as part of a program definition, and how to conduct evaluation to meet the program's mission. This is a major step forward from the traditional accountability systems, which disregard instruction and learning in languages other than English as appropriate for evaluation. As the model reinforces, no matter what kind of program students find themselves in, what they know in their first language is of value to their academic development and provides useful information about their achievement and progress.

The book draws attention to several other aspects of accountability in language education programming that are frequently overlooked. For example, Margo Gottlieb and Diep Nguyen discuss the need to disaggregate data along multiple dimensions, including type of instructional program and the "literacy culture" of students when they enter, to achieve accurate evaluation and understanding of student performance. They also provide specific examples of a process to decide when ELLs should transition to a different type of program or should be redesignated as fluent in English and no longer in need of specialized instruction.

The initial chapters introduce the field of assessment in general. The authors' review of the historical and political context of programming and assessment should be especially helpful to educators new to the field, for the evaluation climate has changed over time, and the history of recent legislation has left an impact on the landscape. Following this historical review, the authors describe research-based principles of assessment that help define the nature, role, and uses of different kinds of data that might be acquired through formal and informal assessments. They define the difference between formative and summative assessment, describe the appropriate uses of each kind of assessment, and offer a comprehensive process for incorporating and balancing them both in an overall framework of assessment. It is especially helpful that their model returns portfolios to the center of assessment and accountability efforts and shows how a portfolio-based approach can be feasible, even under the constraints of current state and federal mandates.

An enjoyable feature of this book is hearing from students and teachers themselves, whose voices are so often missing from books about education. Samples of students' classroom work are included, along with descriptions by their teachers of how they use portfolios every day. The teachers' accounts show beyond any doubt how much they care for their students and their profession. It is to their credit that they are able to put theory into practice in using assessment data to inform instruction and improve student achievement. These chapters on the practice environment move the discussion from the abstract to the real as teachers describe how they actually implement portfolio-based evaluation, and how such evaluations affect day-to-day teaching as well as decision making about instruction.

A common theme in the book is the need for all the adults in a school community to work together to meet the needs of the students. A great strength of the BASIC model is its emphasis on the collaborative nature of the work required to create a comprehensive and inclusive approach to assessment. It is critical that across grade levels, schools, and districts, common types of information be collected and analyzed to provide an appropriate basis for comparison. When educators can agree on common assessments and evidence of student learning, they can then follow students over time with the confidence that all are working from a shared understanding of achievement. The team approach used in SD 54 to bring people together within and across schools shows what can be accomplished, given the vision and the willingness. When everyone understands and accepts the process and agrees on common reference points, the data obtained through evaluation can be used for a wide variety of purposes: to make instructional decisions, to provide a basis for professional development, to inform constituents about individual students' performance, and to judge program effectiveness.

To make the book a real tool for school improvement, the authors provide a wealth of worksheets and tools to help other educators implement their recommendations in any school or district. These resources, which take the form of graphic organizers, timelines, common assessment reference charts, and checklists aligned with the model's framework, help bring the ideas to life. The questions posed in the worksheets also alert educators to aspects of program implementation that need attention so as to provide a high-quality experience for students in all kinds of language education programs. All of the facilitating documents and worksheets are designed to stimulate discussion and analysis of individual schools and districts, and provide the basis for an interactive process that can be used in virtually any school to set the process in motion.

A final note: throughout this Foreword I have been referring, somewhat impersonally, to "the authors." Margo Gottlieb and Diep Nguyen are much more than anonymous writers, however. They are colleagues and friends who have provided support and guidance for my own work over the past two decades. As is abundantly clear from this book, their professional lives are devoted to making a difference for children from diverse linguistic and cultural backgrounds. They respect teachers as intellectually capable decision makers and recognize the real demands made on teachers' time and patience. In their work and personal lives they embody the values of multilingualism and the richness of cross-cultural interaction. Whenever I am fortunate enough to get together with them, as well as with their talented editor, Rebecca Freeman Field, I always know that I have received the gift of time well spent with smart and dedicated women. I fully expect readers to feel the same about the time they spend reading and using this book.

Nancy L. Commins
University of Colorado, Denver

Preface

School administrators and teachers alike face the daunting task of meeting federal and state requirements for large-scale assessment while monitoring students' progress according to local program goals. Although the tests required under the No Child Left Behind Act have improved the visibility of various student subgroups, they do little to help classroom teachers monitor individual students' progress and make instructional modifications on a daily basis. Nichols, Glass, and Berliner (2006), in analyzing the National Assessment of Educational Progress test administered in twenty-five states, concluded that (1) high-stakes testing has a disproportionately negative impact on language-minority students, (2) increased testing pressure is related to increased retention and higher dropout rates, and (3) the occasional performance gains noted are inconsistent. In addition, because mandated state achievement tests are designed with native English-speaking students in mind, they generally are invalid measures of academic achievement for English language learners (ELLs) and so yield information that adversely influences program and classroom instructional decisions.

This book accepts the premise that while large-scale assessments contribute to educational accountability, they should not be the sole factor determining the status of schools, districts, or states. Rather, through a carefully crafted and comprehensive assessment system that values and weighs data from various sources, including data acquired at the classroom, program, district, and state levels, it is possible to gain a more thorough and realistic view of student performance. The system described in this book, which we refer to as the Balanced Assessment and Accountability System, Inclusive and Comprehensive, or BASIC model, provides a practical way for teachers and administrators in language education programs to manage external demands and internal realities simultaneously through the use of well-crafted accountability measures that can serve multiple assessment needs. This model emerged from the cooperation and coordinated effort of many dedicated professionals and has been implemented successfully in a large school district in Illinois.

The Beginning of Collaboration

In 1995, as a new bilingual director on her first few days on the job in a large suburban school district, Diep Nguyen went on a fact-finding mission to understand how ELLs were served. In visiting school after school, she heard teachers expressing concerns about bilingual students who were "not making it." When asked to explain, few teachers could articulate their students' academic strengths and weaknesses. It was also evident that most teachers' comments were based on their informal evaluations of students.

Investigating further, Diep discovered a huge variability in teachers' perceptions of ELLs' capabilities. A student described as excellent by one teacher could be described as "needing bilingual help" by another. Professional disputes often resulted in ELLs being neglected, or dumped on the bilingual teachers, who felt as though they were second-class professionals in their own schools.

Even though the school district used a norm-referenced test of English language proficiency to place and monitor students, it was increasingly difficult to discern what criteria various teachers used to evaluate their students. There were no common criteria for exiting a student from the bilingual program besides the perfunctory "she's ready". It was apparent that the lack of a common assessment framework and practices resulted in students being inappropriately instructed in both the bilingual and general education classrooms across the district.

In a large district of twenty-seven schools, the problem was accentuated by the differences among schools in terms of their approaches to educating ELLs and their instructional foci. The first charge of the new director was to convene a task force to explore ways of restructuring the program. After several months of studying best practices and discussing solutions, the task force agreed that to improve instructional services for ELLs, the program must have common goals and a common assessment plan applicable to all schools in the district.

Diep, needing expert guidance to build this assessment plan, turned to Margo Gottlieb a long-time colleague at the Illinois Resource Center. At their first meeting, in the fall of 1994, they worked out the rudiments of a bilingual pivotal assessment portfolio, which would prove foundational to the district's assessment efforts.

Over the course of a decade of collaboration between the co-authors, the portfolio-based assessment plan eventually evolved into the BASIC model. Throughout this period, Diep was the instructional leader, while Margo served as an outside evaluator and advisor. In 2001, Margo and Diep launched a five-year longitudinal study of the dual-language program based on the data collected in the students' pivotal portfolios. The co-writing of this book represents another stage in the process of two friends helping each other test new ideas and find systemic and practical solutions to assessment and accountability issues confronting language education programs.

Bringing the BASIC Model to Life

The overall purpose of this book is to describe how we developed and implemented our assessment and accountability model with administrators and teachers in language education programs. With this historical and theoretical background in place, we move on to the practicum. We discuss ways to collect evidence of students' learning and achievement using a balanced, practical, portfolio-based approach; share an evaluation framework and results from a longitudinal study; make a case for the thoughtful use of assessment data to improve ELLs' learning; and offer concrete ways for bilingual educators to assess second-language learners, use the results to meet accountability requirements, and build public support for language education programs. We have included an appendix with worksheets to facilitate the implementation of a balanced assessment and accountability system that is inclusive and comprehensive in any educational context.

Much of the information presented this book is the result of ten years of collaboration among central office administrators, principals, and bilingual teachers of the Schaumburg, Illinois, School District 54. These professionals worked in teams at various levels to establish common goals, create and adopt a common pivotal assessment plan, and use assessments to maintain assessment practices relevant to students' learning and aligned with local instructional practices. The questions that were raised at these meetings are presented in this book to guide teams of educators through the collaborative decision-making process that is at the heart of effective implementation of the assessment plan.

This book is meant to inspire discussion and suggest ideas for teachers and administrators of ELLs to use in building a comprehensive assessment model for students in second-language programs. To this end, we show how assessment data can be used alongside contextual information to guide instructional decisions and make program improvements. We also suggest ways for teachers and administrators to manage the internal need for authentic assessment while dealing with the pressures of public accountability and high-stakes testing.

At the time this book goes to press, our colleagues in SD 54 celebrate several noteworthy accomplishments. The dual-language program is in such high demand that additional kindergarten classes are needed to accommodate parents' requests. Four schools that offer the Spanish-English dual-language program have been certified as International Spanish Academies by the Spanish Ministry of Education and Sciences. In addition, the preliminary 2006 state assessment results show that ELLs in the transitional bilingual education program continue to perform above the state average, while ELLs as well native English speakers in the dual-language program outscore their local and state counterparts in grades 4 through 6, meeting or exceeding state academic standards.

The successes encountered in the language education programs of SD 54 are testimony to the fact that teachers and administrators can change the course of children's education and futures in a positive way when we have the political will to do so. When we build an internal assessment and accountability system that focuses primarily on the improvement of teaching and learning, we indeed can provide quality education for all students while simultaneously helping them develop bilingually. As language educators, this vision of "bilingualism for all children" is ultimately what we hold dear to our hearts. We hope that the stories and ideas presented in this book will aid the efforts of educators who believe that bilingualism enriches all children's lives.

Acknowledgments

A book of this sort owes to many. Our first thanks go to Rebecca Freeman Field, colleague and editor, for her steady encouragement throughout our collaboration and her vision for this project. Under her guidance, the book underwent numerous transformations to reach its present form. We are also deeply grateful to the bilingual teachers and students of the Schaumburg, Illinois, School District 54. The BASIC Model was first implemented in their classrooms, and we learned much from the evaluations in which they willingly participated. In particular, teachers and coordinators Naseem Alibhai, Rocio Hernandez, Danette Meyer, Magali Williams, and Barbara Wojtysiak, whose contributions appear in Chapters 5 and 6, deserve special plaudits. On the larger stage, all past and current members of the Bilingual Education Support Team of SD 54 helped shape an environment in which bilingual education could thrive. We are glad to say that Ed Rafferty, superintendent of SD 54, was an enthusiastic supporter of the project from the start. We benefited much from his involvement and appreciate his generosity in allowing us to feature the work of the bilingual staff of of SD 54.

Our husbands, Terry Gottleib and Bill Shaw, and our children, Graham, Tim, Daniel, and Ian, were understanding when we needed time to write and let us know in countless ways how much they love us. We cherish that love, and return it.

Contents

Chapter **8**   **Making It Work in Your Language Education Program: Lessons from the Field**   **173**

Assessment and Accountability in Language Education Programs: National and Local Perspectives

Chapter Overview

This opening chapter discusses the stark change in demographics of the school-aged population in the United States, with emphasis on English language learners, and it provides an historical overview of language education programs. We then examine the pragmatics of configuring language education programs based on externally imposed constraints and internal, local influences as the backdrop for assessment and accountability. The chapter closes with an introduction to a school district, highlighted throughout the book, which has spearheaded the development and implementation of a cohesive, coordinated, and collaborative assessment and accountability system for its language education programs.

Guiding Questions

- How have language education programs and the students they serve changed over time?
- What are some influences that are instrumental in shaping language education programs?
- How has your school or district responded to the language education needs of its students?

Key Concepts

- Externally imposed accountability requirements for the academic achievement of all children focus attention on English language learners.
- The increasing numbers of English language learners in schools brings attention to language education programs.
- Language education programs are influenced by internal and external forces.
- Local school districts and schools can make a difference in the language education of their students.

The integration of assessment and accountability into the school culture over the past decade has been felt particularly in the language education community. Never before have the teachers and administrators of language programs had to deal with issues and policies where proof of program success has made such a difference to the children served.

This chapter provides the foundation for the discussion in subsequent chapters of assessment and accountability in language education programs in the United States today. We begin at the national level and review the types of bilingual, English-only, and world language programs offered to English language learners (ELLs) and English speakers in U.S. schools. Then we introduce the language education programs and practices in Schaumburg Community Consolidated School District 54 in Schaumburg, Illinois, the case study that illustrates the assessment and accountability system presented in this book. We call this system the BASIC model, where BASIC stands for Balanced Assessment and Accountability System, Inclusive and Comprehensive. This model is grounded in contextual information, framed by learning standards, goals, and benchmarks, and responsive to four levels of accountability (state, district, program and classroom). It offers a framework for educators who are working to develop authentic assessment and accountability systems in their language education programs.

The National Level: Goals and Challenges for Language Education Programs

Language education in the United States and worldwide has seen something of a renaissance in the past decade. Three major forces have shaped the emergence of language programming as a core part of the school experience. The first is the growing need for multilingual, multicultural competence in the global community, the second is the increasing number of immigrants arriving in the United States, and the third is recognition of the imminent loss of minority or heritage languages, and efforts to recuperate them (Lindholm-Leary, 2001). These reasons have compelled educators to examine how best to improve teaching to better serve students through language education programs.

The shifting demographics of school-aged children in the United States, coupled with the growing demands for accountability for learning, have raised the awareness of educators of how to effectively approach the education of language-minority and language-majority students (Freeman, Freeman, & Mecuri, 2005). In the 2003–04 school year, of the total school enrollment of almost 50 million students, approximately 5 million ELLs were being served in language education programs. Even as the total school enrollment grew by about 9% over the last decade, the ELL population grew by an astounding 65% during the same period (National Clearinghouse for English Language Acquisition, 2005). Additionally, proficient English-speaking students are increasingly enrolling in language education programs, such as foreign language at the elementary school (FLES) programs, dual language programs, or enrichment classes. Some of these English speakers are heritage language speakers who use a language other than English (i.e., their heritage language) at home. According to U.S. Census 2000 data, an estimated 9.9 million of the 45 million school-aged children live in households in which a language other than English is spoken (Lindholm-Leary, 2001). These statistics point to the need for a national dialogue about the complex issues educators face in today's classrooms. Additionally, it is imperative to develop some means of capitalizing on our rich linguistic resources at hand.

Language Education Services and Programs

English language learners are a subset of linguistically and culturally diverse students who, by definition, need language support to reach parity with their proficient English peers. There are currently two main approaches to language education programs for ELLs: bilingual education and English-only education. Bilingual education means using two languages for instructional purposes, and English-only education means that only English is used. Each approach is addressed by multiple program types. Although there has been discussion about eliminating programmatic models, in U.S. public schools today, the same instructional models tend to recur across various educational settings (Miramontes, Nadeau, & Commins, 1997).

Under the bilingual education umbrella are dual language, one-way developmental bilingual education, and transitional bilingual education programs. In dual language or two-way immersion (TWI) programs, ELLs and English speakers learn together in integrated classes, with both groups receiving content area instruction in two languages. One-way developmental or maintenance bilingual programs target ELLs and heritage language speakers and promote the development of students' first or heritage language while they learn academic English and academic content through two languages. Both one-way developmental and two-way immersion programs can be understood as developmental bilingual programs because their goals include bilingualism and biliteracy development for their target populations. Transitional bilingual education (TBE) programs provide students with English as a second language (ESL) instruction and academic support in the students' native language, with native language instruction gradually decreasing and eventually eliminated as ELLs acquire more and more English. Early-exit TBE programs encourage a fast transition to English-only education and typically last one to three years, while late-exit TBE programs generally provide services to ELLs for three to five years.

The English-only approach to ELLs' language education includes programs that are called either ESL or English language development (ELD). These programs should include two major components: sheltered content instruction, so that ELLs learn academic content in English, and ESL instruction, so that they develop the English language proficiency they need to participate and achieve in the all-English academic mainstream. Schools vary in the ways they design their ESL or ELD programs for ELLs, depending largely on the numbers of ELLs they serve.

The primary goal of both transitional bilingual programs and ESL/ELD programs is to facilitate ELLs' transition to all-English classrooms as soon as possible. These types of programs generally have three goals: (1) acquiring English language proficiency, (2) achieving academically in English, and (3) making a successful sociocultural transition into American schools. Developmental bilingual programs have the additional goals of developing bilingualism (in oral language, literacy, and content) and cross-cultural competence for their target populations, which include but are not limited to ELLs.

Other types of language education programs aim to enrich English speakers' proficiency in other languages. For example, under the developmental bilingual education umbrella, we find foreign language immersion programs that share common goals with dual language/TWI and one-way developmental bilingual programs. We find foreign or world language programs that teach a target language, such as Chinese, French, or German, as a subject of instruction; at the elementary level these are known as FLES (foreign language in the elementary school) programs. We also find heritage language programs, which aim to broaden the linguistic repertoire of heritage language speakers and strengthen their linguistic and cultural identity. The most common example of heritage language programs in K–12 schools today are Spanish for Spanish speakers programs. Table 1.1 summarizes the goals and characteristics of these types of language education programs.

A variety of students participate in language education programs from early childhood through the high school years. Some have never been exposed to English, others may never have had an opportunity to acquire an additional language outside of English. Still others may have oral facility in their native language or knowledge of cultural traditions from their family backgrounds, and wish to further develop their language skills. Table 1.2 identifies students and the types of language programs in which they participate. This table is useful for language educators who are considering the kinds of language education program options available for their student population. {Table 1.2}

Although these two tables tend to perpetuate the notion of models of language education programs and the learners served, in reality, they represent a continuum of services, from those that represent a strong infusion of native language for instruction to those that use native language more sparingly for support to those in which English is the sole medium of instruction. In their totality, these program alternatives have evolved to meet the diverse and complex needs of language learners in the United States today (Christian, 2006).

Historical Overview of Language Education Programs

The launch of *Sputnik* in 1957 and the sharp awakening of the United States to the achievements of foreign governments and scientists delivered an unprecedented boost to foreign language study in the United States. The early programs were managed under a Department of Defense title as "critical foreign languages" and were intended for students proficient in English. Not long after, bilingual education programs for students who were not proficient in English were initiated. In 1963, the Coral Way Elementary School in Florida responded to the educational needs of Cuban children who had begun arriving in the early 1960s by establishing a bilingual school. Coral Way Elementary School started the first dual language program in the United States promotes the development of bilingualism and biliteracy for its ELLs and English speakers.

Table 1.1 Features of Language Education Programs

Approach to Language Education	Type of Language Education Program	Goals	Distinguishing Characteristics
Developmental bilingual education	Dual language/ two-way immersion	• Bilingualism and biliteracy • Academic achievement in two languages • Cross-cultural competence	• Serve ELLs from a common language background alongside proficient English speakers. • As much of 90% in L1, 10% in L2, diminishing to 50/50 ratio over time.
	One-way developmental/maintenance bilingual education	• Bilingualism and biliteracy • Academic achievement in two languages • Cross-cultural competence	• Serve ELLs and heritage language speakers from a common language background. • As much of 90% in L1, 10% in L2, moving to 50/50 ratio over time.
	Foreign language immersion	• Bilingualism and biliteracy • Academic achievement in two languages • Cross-cultural competence	• Serve English speakers (or students from language backgrounds other than the target language). • As much of 90% in L1, 10% in L2, moving to 50/50 ratio over time.
Transitional bilingual education	Late-exit transitional bilingual programs	• English language proficiency • Academic achievement in English • Acculturation into U.S. society	• Serve ELLs from a common language background. • Instruction in L1 diminishes over time until L2 is used exclusively. • Students generally participate in the program for more than three years.

Table 1.1 *continues*

Approach to Language Education	Type of Language Education Program	Goals	Distinguishing Characteristics
Transitional bilingual education (*continued*)	Early-exit transitional bilingual programs	• English language proficiency • Academic achievement in English • Acculturation into U.S. society	• Serve ELLs from a common language background. • Instruction in L1 diminishes over time until L2 is used exclusively. • Program participation is generally limited to one to three years.
English only	English as a Second Language (ESL)/ English language development (ELD)	• English language proficiency • Academic achievement in English • Acculturation into U.S. society	• Serve ELLs. • Provide instruction in English, sometimes with (minimal) L1 support.
Additional approaches to language enrichment	Foreign/ world language education	• Target language proficiency • Cultural awareness and cross-cultural understanding	• Serve proficient English speakers. • Develop oral language and literacy in a language other than English.
	Heritage language programs (e.g., Spanish for Spanish speakers)	• Oral and written skills in the target heritage language • Positive cultural identity	• Serve heritage language students. • Broaden linguistic repertoire. • Validate linguistic and cultural identity of heritage language speakers.

Table 1.2 Student Participation in Language Education Programs

Students	Language Education Program Options
English language learners (ELLs) Linguistically and culturally diverse students who need language support to reach parity with their English-proficient peers.	• Dual language/two-way immersion • One-way developmental bilingual • Transitional bilingual • ESL or ELD • Heritage language (e.g., Gujarati for Gujarati speakers)
Heritage language speakers Students who speak a language other than English at home, with varying degrees of proficiency; these students are (generally) proficient English speakers but not necessarily literate in a language other than English	• Heritage language (e.g., Gujarati for Gujarati speakers) • Dual language/two-way immersion • One-way developmental bilingual
Proficient English learners Former ELLs who have transitioned from English language support services	• Dual language/two-way immersion • Foreign language immersion • Heritage language • Foreign/world language courses (for a language other than their heritage language)
Native English speakers Students whose language background is English	• Dual language/two-way immersion • Foreign language immersion • Foreign/world language courses

Over the next ten years, legal precedent for bilingual education in the United States was set by the Civil Rights Act of 1964, followed by the Bilingual Education Acts of 1968 and 1974, in which federal monies first became available to support bilingual education programs. The Equal Educational Opportunity Act of 1974 and the Supreme Court ruling in *Lau v. Nichols* that same year firmly established the requirement of appropriate language support in the schooling of language-minority students. These decisions were upheld in a flurry of court cases that followed, beginning with *Castañeda v. Pickard* in 1981, which set the precedent for the courts in examining programs for ELLs. This programmatic standard requires language education services for ELLs to pass a three-pronged test: (1) programs for ELLs must be based on an educational theory recognized as sound by experts; (2) resources, personnel, and practices must be reasonably calculated to implement the program effectively; and (3) programs must be evaluated and, if necessary, restructured to ensure that language barriers are overcome (see Crawford, 2006, for further discussion).

In the 1980s, following the example of immersion education in Canada, a few experimental language-immersion education programs were begun in the United States. The students enrolled in these programs typically represented a language-majority group—most often native English speakers—and thus developed their first language naturally at home and in the community, while at school they were immersed in a target second language, such as French, for instruction. Studies of the Canadian immersion programs showed that students who received instruction strictly in the target second language succeeded in becoming bilingual and achieving academically in two languages (Genesee, 1985; Lambert & Tucker, 1972).

During the 1990s, inspired by the success of the Canadian models, U.S. legislators committed federal dollars to developing dual language or two-way immersion programs in the United States. Funds also became available for foreign language education. Today, a myriad of different services support language development.

Much of the research on language development and learning has focused on the comparative effectiveness of different program models and instructional practices within language education. Howard and Sugarman (2001) and Lindholm-Leary (2001) assert that ELLs who participate in dual language programs develop bilingual proficiency as well as strong academic skills. In a longitudinal national study on the effectiveness of program models for language-minority students, Thomas and Collier (1997, 2002) and Collier and Thomas (2004) also found that although ELLs in ESL programs make quick gains in English proficiency, it is the developmental bilingual education programs such as dual language and late-exit TBE programs that have lasting positive effects on ELLs' achievement.

Influences on Language Education Programs

Educational programs do not operate in isolation, and language education programs are no exception. There is a confluence of external and internal forces that help shape the very nature of the services provided. A consideration of these influences is the starting point for planning language education program development and for developing authentic assessment and accountability systems for those programs.

External Influences

Several factors that affect how language education programs are conceived and perceived are largely outside the control of the local school or school district. Typically, language education policies enacted at the national or state level lead to policies being imposed at the local and regional levels. Several states have banned the use of native language for instructional purposes, for example, while others, conversely, require schools to offer a variety of bilingual education services, depending on the density and homogeneity of the language of the students.

A second consideration is the composition and distribution of the student population, that is, the characteristics of the students themselves. Language education programs provided in neighborhood schools must respond to the needs of the specific student population within that neighborhood. For example, in some areas there is a growing preschool language-minority population from one or more language groups, while other areas have seen an influx of older students from nations disrupted by war, whose formal schooling was limited or interrupted. The language education services provided in the first neighborhood are quite different from those provided in the second.

A third factor is the participation and support of the community at large. The extent to which parents and community groups enter the conversation and become involved in the formulation of language education programs makes a difference in how the programs are conceptualized. The influences of student and community characteristics and constituents on the formation of language education programs are explained in greater detail in Chapter 2.

Internal Influences

A coherent language education program depends on the positive interaction of the various sources of input to that program. First, theory and research inform the learning standards, goals, and benchmarks to be addressed, and those standards, goals, and benchmarks in turn dictate the

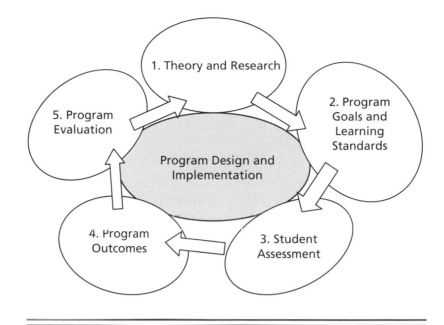

Figure 1.1   Relationship among internal influences on program design and implementation.

types of assessments to be used. In a standards-driven program, student assessment provides evidence of programmatic outcomes whose effectiveness is demonstrated through program evaluation. Figure 1.1 shows the relationship among these sources of input in program design, implementation, and refinement.

Worksheet 1 in the Appendix asks educators to identify the sources of influence that affect their language education program design, and Worksheet 2 surveys the degree to which this input is considered in program implementation and refinement. Explicit attention to each of these sources of influence helps program leaders align the language education program with the *Castañeda* standard (i.e., the programs are pedagogically sound, well-implemented, and deliver results).

Assessment Requirements within Language Education Programs

Although assessment has always been a part of language education programs (such as for the identification, placement, and reclassification of ELLs), the use of language proficiency and academic achievement data, anchored in state standards, for accountability purposes stems directly from the No Child Left Behind (NCLB) legislation of 2001 (Gottlieb,

2006). This reauthorization of the Elementary and Secondary School Act requires states to conduct annual, summative assessments of academic achievement for all students in grades 3 through 8, and once for students in high school. Assessment is required minimally in English language arts/reading, mathematics, and science, in benchmark grade levels. In addition, English language proficiency assessment is to be administered to ELLs in grade levels K–12.

The impact of this federal mandate has been widely felt in the bilingual education community as it tends to favor demonstration of academic achievement in English and, for the most part, does not account for academic learning gains in the students' native language. Bilingual educators struggle to meet public accountability requirements for academic proficiency in English while maintaining native language instruction and assessment. Meanwhile, the results of yearly tests have been used to compare students' achievement by designated subgroups, including gender, race, socioeconomic status, special needs, and ELL status. Stringent guidelines for meeting Adequate Yearly Progress (AYP) requirements have been imposed by states based on these data, causing many programs to abandon developmental and TBE programs in favor of English-only models. These programs have been abandoned despite strong convergent evidence from a recent comprehensive synthesis of the empirically based research on the achievement of ELLs (Genesee et al, in press) that the educational success of ELLs is positively related to sustained instruction through the student's first language (Lindholm-Leary, 2006)

During these contentious times in education, conversations among practitioners center on how we can use valid assessment to inform our own instructional decisions and simultaneously address the pressure of public accountability mandates under a generally unfavorable political climate for bilingual education. Educators need to gather evidence from multiple sources throughout the year so that data are available for defending decision making. In language education, it is important to examine and share examples of assessment plans that have proved effective in schools, and to present balanced, practical assessment and evaluation frameworks that are replicable in language education programs in other school settings. There is also a need to present empirical evidence of students' growth and achievement in different types of well-implemented language education programs as a way to ground the national conversation about what types of programs are most effective for language learners. The work of a school district to address these challenges became the impetus for writing this book.

A Local Perspective: Assessment and Accountability in Language Education Programs in Schaumburg School District 54

The experience of Schaumburg Community Consolidated School District 54 offers a rich case study in the collaborative development of an assessment plan for a district with a broad demographic profile. School District 54 is located in a northwestern suburb of Chicago and serves pre-kindergarten through eighth-grade students from five neighboring townships. The Schaumburg area, originally settled by German immigrants and farmers, today is a thriving suburb with many retail and international businesses. The district includes 21 elementary schools (K–6), five junior high schools (7–8), and one K–8 school of choice. It also has a parent-paid preschool program and a preschool program for students with disabilities.

School District 54 is the second largest elementary school district in Illinois, after the City of Chicago. The 14,000 students attending the schools in this district come from diverse linguistic, cultural, and socioeconomic backgrounds. They speak more than 40 different languages at home. About 10 percent are identified as ELLs. The ELL population has increased by approximately 100 students annually for the past decade even as the general school enrollment has decreased over the same period. Figure 1.2 shows the decrease in general student enrollment in comparison to the increase in ELL enrollment over the past 12 years, a trend repeated throughout the United States over the last decade.

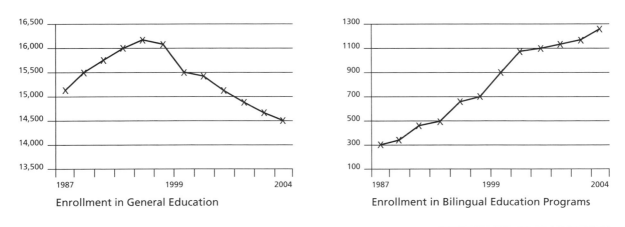

Figure 1.2 Enrollment trends in School District 54 in general education and bilingual education programs over the past 12 years.

Language Education Program Mission

The mission of the language education programs of School District 54 was developed in 1995 by a task force attempting to restructure the bilingual education program, and it remains the same to this day. The mission is "to provide opportunities, experiences and instruction to enable all students to learn successfully and be full participants in their respective and diverse school communities while developing bilingual proficiencies."

The goals of the language education programs are:

* To facilitate students' learning of English as a second language and other second languages

* To enable students to learn academic subjects through bilingual instruction

* To help students develop intercultural communication and collaborative problem solving skills

* To foster students' independence as well as interdependence as members of a community of learners

School District 54's mission and program goals provide overall guidance in the development of the different language education programs offered in the district as well as the local assessment plan that was developed.

Language Education Programs in School District 54

The district provides an interconnected system of support for a diverse group of second language learners in all its 27 schools. The system includes (1) a comprehensive, gradual-exit, TBE program from kindergarten through grade 8, serving English language learners from more than 18 language groups; (2) a dual language program of choice in Spanish-English from kindergarten through grade 8 at four schools, and a dual language program of choice in Japanese-English currently in kindergarten through grade 4 at one elementary school; and (3) a FLES program in Spanish and Japanese at six elementary schools, and foreign/world language classes in French and Spanish at all junior high schools. Each of these programs is described in more detail below.

Transitional Bilingual Education Program

The TBE program started in 1973 with a handful of students receiving itinerant services. Today the program serves students from more than 20 language backgrounds in both self-contained and resource classrooms, where services gradually diminish as students gain English language proficiency. The three major components of the TBE program are (1) instruction in English as a second language, (2) native language support for academic content learning, and (3) assistance in making the cultural transition into the general education setting. In the primary grades, students in self-contained TBE classes develop native language literacy as they simultaneously acquire English. At the upper grade levels, ELLs are integrated into general education classes for part of the day and receive ESL instruction and native language support from a bilingual teacher and bilingual assistants the remainder of the day. Figure 1.3 outlines the bilingual individual instructional plan (BIIP) that guides instruction for ELLs in grades 1 through 8.

Bilingual instructional assistants are an integral part of the teaching staff. They provide native language support for a multilingual group of students as well as individualized and small-group instruction. Typically, there is a bilingual instructional assistant in every bilingual classroom. To integrate students more successfully into general education classrooms and to build overall staff capacity to serve ELLs, beginning in 1999, the school district established a practice of filling general education teaching positions with certified content teachers who are fluent English speakers and who also have at least intermediate proficiency in other languages, resulting in the creation of a job category called English+ teachers. Though not formally trained in ESL or bilingual methods, all English+ teachers are encouraged to pursue an ESL endorsement (18 graduate hours across six courses) as part of their tenure procurement. ELLs who are almost ready to transition from the TBE program are placed in these classes alongside their native English-speaking peers. The ability of these teachers to shelter instruction and offer native language support for individual students has contributed significantly to the successful, gradual transition of students from the TBE program.

As evidenced in the Illinois State Board of Education's Report Cards from 2003–2006, statewide assessment results have shown that ELLs in School District 54 consistently outperform other ELLs in the state on measures of reading, writing, and math. The 2005 follow-up school dis-

Student's Name _____   **School Year** _____

Teacher's Name _____   **Grade Level** _____

	ESL/ Language Arts	Social Studies*	Science*	Math*	Specials
ESL I	Native language literacy and content-based ESL	Monolingual English instruction with native language support *or* bilingual instruction in the Bilingual Resource Room	Hands-on science in monolingual English classroom with native language support *or* bilingual instruction in the Bilingual Resource Room	Monolingual English instruction with native language support *or* bilingual instruction in the Bilingual Resource Room	Monolingual English instruction with native language support when necessary
ESL II	Content-based ESL and transition into English literacy	Monolingual English instruction with native language support	Hands-on science in monolingual English classroom with native language support	Monolingual English instruction with native language support	Monolingual English instruction with native language support when necessary
ESL III	ESL support in Bilingual Resource Room (minimal or no content-based ESL) Language Arts in English	Monolingual English instruction with minimal native language support	Monolingual English instruction with minimal native language support	Monolingual English instruction with minimal native language support	Monolingual English instruction
Transition	All instruction in the monolingual English classroom	All instruction in the monolingual English classroom	All instruction in the monolingual English classroom	All instruction in the monolingual English classroom	All instruction in the monolingual English classroom

*Academic content instruction must be adapted to meet the needs of each student.

Dates

_____   1st Trimester Plan: Put **1** in each appropriate box.

_____   2nd Trimester Plan: Put **2** in each appropriate box.

_____   3rd Trimester Plan: Put **3** in each appropriate box.

Figure 1.3   Bilingual individual instructional plan (BIIP), a bilingual resource for first through eighth graders. (Schaumburg Community Consolidated School District 54, Schaumburg, Illinois; reprinted with permission)

trict study conducted on ELLs who exited the TBE program after one, two, and three years found that 90% to 95% of these students continued to be successful in their studies.

Dual Language Program

In 1995, as School District 54 embarked on restructuring its bilingual services to ELLs, the establishment of a dual language program became a top priority. Federal funds helped establish the first cohort of Spanish-English dual language classrooms at one school, thus inaugurating the first program of choice for families in the district. In 2000, parents urged that the model be replicated at another school, followed by a third site in 2003. As of 2006, the Spanish-English dual language program has served 380 students from kindergarten through eighth grade.

The dual language program utilizes an 80/20 instructional model with an emphasis on native language literacy first for all students. Accordingly, in kindergarten, 80% of instruction is delivered in Spanish and 20% in English. The allocation of the language of instruction is adjusted in subsequent grades until a balance of 50/50 is reached in fifth grade and maintained in sixth grade. At the junior high school level, former dual language students attend two courses daily that are taught entirely in Spanish. In 2003, the Japanese-English dual language program was established, using a 50/50 model at one elementary school. As of 2006, this program has served 108 students and, like its English-Spanish counterpart, continues to grow.

In 2004 the school district, in collaboration with the Illinois Resource Center, became the Midwest school demonstration site for Project Dual U, a Web-based staff development program that provides training to administrators and teachers embarking on dual language education around the country. Teachers and administrators who attend Dual U in the Midwest visit School District 54 to observe dual language classes in action.

In 2002, School District 54 conducted an evaluation study of its dual language program using longitudinal data on student performance. Chapter 7 presents the findings of this study, which demonstrate the effectiveness for ELLs and English speakers in the program. Although not part of a formal evaluation study, test results from the 2005–06 academic year demonstrate that ELLs in the dual language program closed the gap with their English-speaking counterparts in School District 54 (see Chapter 5 for further discussion of these data).

Table 1.3 SD 54's 2005–2006 Second Language Program Enrollment Figures

Language Program	Grade Levels Served	No. Enrolled
Transitional bilingual education	K–8	1,142
Dual language: Spanish-English	K–8	380
Dual language: Japanese-English	K–4	108
Foreign language in elementary schools	K–6	1,590
Foreign/world language courses	7–8	1,927
Total No. of students in language education programs (K–8)		**5,147**

Foreign Language in the Elementary School and Foreign Language Classes

School District 54 has implemented a FLES program in seven schools, and the program is expanding every year. Locally developed formative assessments and benchmarks are used to measure student progress in this program. The FLES facilitator and the dual language facilitator collaborate on a regular basis in staff development activities. In addition, foreign/world language courses in French and Spanish are offered at all of the junior high schools. Table 1.3 summarizes the number of second language learners in each type of language education program during the 2005–06 school year.

Local Assessment Practices

Internal accountability of a district's language education programs relies on a comprehensive and rigorous assessment plan for each student. Long before NCLB imposed external accountability demands on local schools, School District 54 had developed a comprehensive assessment framework to address its own internal accountability requirements.

The following critical questions provided direction as the staff of School District 54 built the common assessment plan used in their language education programs:

- What are the goals for the second language learners in our program? Are these goals aligned with State and District learning standards and the program's mission? Do they include language development, academic achievement, and cross-cultural competence?

- How are second language learners functioning in each of the core academic subjects in relation to the specified program goals? What criteria are used to determine the extent to which every student meets these benchmarks within the program?

- What evidence needs to be collected to show that second language students have acquired the skills and knowledge required to achieve expected academic achievement and language proficiency in a particular core content subject? Does the evidence give authentic and valid information about students' learning?

- Does the program have a common assessment framework and a plan to help teams of teachers collaboratively collect data in order to monitor students' progress? Is this plan aligned with the district instructional goals and practices as well as state standards?

- Is this plan balanced in providing practitioners with information that is useful to make day-to-day instructional decisions as well as helping to inform administrators of long-range achievement made by students as a whole? How can this information be used for continuous program improvement?

- Is the common assessment plan well articulated and shared by all constituents? Is the assessment timeline manageable for both teachers and students?

- Do groups of teachers have opportunities to explore and create common assessments to be included in the plan that are practical and fair for their students? What part of the comprehensive assessment plan is negotiable, and which part should be mandated for all teachers?

Originally designed with bilingual teachers and students in mind, School District 54's comprehensive portfolio-based assessment plan provides all teachers with information about individual students' growth and achievement relative to the goals of the language education program, and that information is gathered from multiple sources. This portfolio includes results from formative and summative assessments of student learning across content areas in two languages. It also contains authentic student work samples and common or standard assessments in core learning areas, and thus serves as a tool for monitoring progress and planning instruction and learning goals. In addition, it provides critical data for program evaluation and improvement.

At least three times a year, teams of teachers share their students' portfolios to plan for instruction. The portfolio is cumulative in that it follows students from year to year throughout their participation in the bilingual program. Upon exit or graduation, test results are purged and the collection of student work is bound and given to the student as a gift and testimony of the student's participation. More than just a record of growth and achievement, the portfolio is a rich portrait of each student's individual learning and a historical archive of his or her accomplishments.

The People behind the Assessment Plan: The Importance of Collaboration

> *There is no doubt that a small group of committed people can work to change the world. Indeed, it's the only thing that ever did.*
>
> —Margaret Mead

This book is as much about building a comprehensive assessment plan as it is about the collaborative work that makes it happen. The successful implementation of the district's assessment system can be attributed to a team approach used at every level to make decisions throughout the past decade.

The author's collaboration, which is ongoing, has been sustained through many program stages, from the inception and design of School District 54's assessment framework, to continuous dialogues and consultation during the implementation and improvement of the assessment plan, to the longitudinal study to evaluate the dual language program, to the development of the BASIC model that emerged from the grounded work in School District 54, and eventually to the co-authoring of this book.

At the same time, the staff in the school district has implemented and improved the assessment plan using a team approach at the school level as well as the program level. This team effort has resulted in a common purpose and culture for a group of teachers who were isolated and disenfranchised, and in addition has created group ownership of the assessment and instructional plan. The collaborative approach that the language education professionals in School District 54 take has been a driving force in all of their work for over ten years, and it is aligned with what is known as professional learning communities (DuFour, DuFour, Eaker, & Karhanek 2004).

After 12 years of program restructuring and staff development, collaborative work has become the norm for bilingual teachers in School District 54. Today, there are different teams that perform various functions at various levels.

Language Program Administrative Team

The language program administrative team consists of two administrators, two assessment teachers, one program evaluation specialist, one dual language facilitator, and one bilingual literacy specialist. The team is responsible for the day-to-day operation of all second language programs in the district. In addition to their specialized duties, they participate in local school leadership and on resource teams, and provide daily assistance to local schools to help ensure quality education for all students.

The Bilingual Education Support Team (BESTeam)

The BESTeam is the leadership team of the bilingual education program. It consists of two administrators and seven lead teachers who are experts in their fields of interests and become mentors to new bilingual teachers. The BESTeam meets monthly to evaluate, on a formative basis, different aspects of the program, to plan common staff development, and to make subtle program improvements. Each member of the team also provides guidance to other teachers, teaches workshops and classes related to language education, and serves as the chairperson for a team of job-alike bilingual teachers.

Bilingual Job-Alike Teams

Each bilingual classroom teacher participates on a bilingual job-alike team that meets once a month to articulate and communicate strategies that best fit the needs of second language learners. Staff development is differentiated by team. There are five job-alike bilingual teacher teams: TBE junior high school, TBE elementary resource (for native Spanish speakers), TBE elementary resource (for other language groups), TBE primary self-contained (K–2 for native Spanish speakers), and dual language (Spanish-English and Japanese-English). All the bilingual instructional assistants also have their own team that meets on a monthly basis.

School-Level Teams

At each school, bilingual teachers also participate in their grade-level articulation team and the special education child study teams. In addition, many are members of the school leadership team.

District-Level Teams

Because the bilingual department of the district is a part of the special services area, the two bilingual administrators are members of district-level teams that meet weekly to articulate issues and share decision making on matters related to bilingual and special education students. They also are members of the district-wide administrative team that meets on a quarterly basis with the superintendent. In addition, many bilingual teachers participate on district-wide curriculum and leadership teams, where they advocate for the interests of second language learners.

It is through this network of teams that decisions about assessment are posed and clarified before implementation. Critical program decisions are often made only after several discussions, with input provided from various teams. Figure 1.4 illustrates the relationship between the network of teams responsible for implementation of the assessment plan in School District 54.

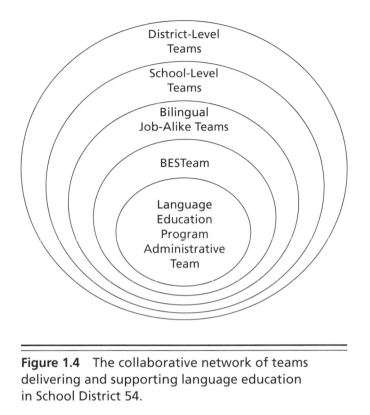

Figure 1.4 The collaborative network of teams delivering and supporting language education in School District 54.

Integrating National and Local Perspectives: Introducing the BASIC Model

At the national level, assessment and accountability of our educational programs are skeletal, because criteria for data collection, analysis, and reporting need to be adaptable so as to apply to diverse states and territories. Quality standards are to align with and drive assessment, which in large part represents summative, large-scale efforts. Assessment must be of high technical rigor because the stakes are high. For language education programs with ELLs, accountability rests on dual sets of standards and assessments. The connection between language proficiency and academic achievement must be clear, yet measurement of the constructs must remain distinct.

At the local level, school districts have the option of taking a state's assessment and accountability plan and crafting a full-bodied system, as in the case of School District 54's language education program. As long as the system is in compliance with federal and state requirements, the expertise and experience of teachers and administrators should be paramount in the design of valid and viable systems. Student and program data from multiple sources, gathered on a formative and summative basis, offer continuous insight into teaching and learning. Assessment and accountability become contextualized, meaningful to all constituents, and useful as input for the continual improvement of language services.

This book presents what we call the BASIC model, which stands for a Balanced Assessment and Accountability System, Inclusive and Comprehensive. The BASIC model is authentic in that it draws on language education program goals and state learning standards as the backdrop for acquiring mutually agreed-upon formative data on students and classrooms. Its authenticity is also derived from consensus and decision making on the part of constituents, including students, parents, teachers, and administrators. The model is balanced and comprehensive in that state summative assessments are complemented with formative assessments to gain full insight into the performance of students or classes. These assessment data represent a wealth of sources, from teacher observation of individual students to secure large-scale tests. Finally, the BASIC model is inclusive, built from a set of assessment principles, designed to reflect exemplary services of language education programs.

Questions for Reflection and Action

1. Investigate the student demographics of your school or school district over the past several decades (for example, total number of students and breakdown by language groups, SES, and other variables). What are some of the trends you detect and how might your predict future patterns?

2. Think about the influences that affect the language education program at your school, district, or state. How would you rank them in terms of their potential impact (both negative and positive)?

How might you mitigate the more detrimental forces and accentuate the more positive ones?

3. Reflect on your role within your local language education program. Name 3–5 actions you might take to advocate on its behalf, irrespective of whether or not you are in philosophic agreement with how it functions.

2

The BASIC Model for Language Education Programs

Chapter Overview

This chapter introduces five assessment principles that lead to strong language education programs and serve as the foundation for the BASIC model. We describe in detail the components of the model and how they work together within a system. In addition, we recognize and honor each community's defining features, student characteristics, and educational policies as the context in which the BASIC model operates.

Guiding Questions

- What do you believe are important principles or precepts for student assessment in your setting?
- Are there any theoretical models that guide your assessment and instruction? If so, which ones and what are their components?
- What is the context in which instructional and assessment practices of language education programs function within your school, district, or state?

Key Concepts

- Assessment principles lay the groundwork for assessment models, frameworks and systems.
- Theoretical models, such as the BASIC model, help organize and explain evidence of teaching and learning.
- Curriculum, instruction, and assessment are at the core of the BASIC model, and they are framed by learning standards, goals and benchmarks and grounded in contextual information.
- The BASIC model relies on different types of assessment for different purposes, and is responsive to classroom, program, district, and state accountability requirements.

For language education programs that seek to continuously improve, accountability is as much internally driven by teachers and administrators working on the classroom, program, and school levels as it is externally imposed by district and state policies and accountability requirements. To achieve a balance among the potentially competing forces of internal and external accountability, planning for assessment should be a deliberate, meaningful process. This chapter addresses the critical question, how can school districts and schools balance the internal and external accountability requirements of language education programs? In response, we describe what we call the BASIC model, the acronym for a Balanced Assessment and Accountability System, Inclusive and Comprehensive. The BASIC model balances the often competing forces of internal and external accountability by including approaches for collecting, analyzing, and interpreting data from multiple sources, and by promoting the thoughtful, fair, and appropriate use of such data to make sound educational decisions on the classroom, program, district, and state levels of implementation. Assessment practices that balance and integrate different types of data from multiple sources for different purposes are grounded in principles of assessment, and they are systemic and function within operational frameworks. The data generated within such frameworks provide the evidence for rational decision making in language education programs.

Principles of Assessment in Language Education Programs

Several fundamental principles defining the role of assessment and the use of data in language education programs provide the foundation for the BASIC model. Derived from research and theory, these principles guide the formation and maintenance of sound, authentic assessment and accountability systems. These principles may be used as markers for language education in lieu of trying to fit programs to specified models.

Assessment Principle 1. Teaching and learning are influenced by the interaction among learning goals, learning standards, and learning benchmarks, and their alignment with assessment measures.

The key to Assessment Principle 1 is alignment, or the degree of correspondence between two entities; this connection may be considered weak, moderate, or strong. In creating language education programs, there needs to be a deliberate matching of learning goals, learning standards, and learning benchmarks with assessment measures. The overlap among these components is a source of strength and validity of any educational program.

All K–12 public educational systems in the United States are grounded in learning standards that define what is expected of students. Each state's academic content standards spell out the knowledge and skills that every student needs to know and be able to do in each core curricular area. These standards provide a reference point or benchmark for measures of academic achievement.

For language education programs serving English language learners (ELLs), there are also state English language proficiency standards that delineate the language requisite for social interaction and the language of the content areas—minimally, language arts, mathematics, and science. The performance indicators for each English language proficiency level outline the pathways to language development across the language domains of listening, speaking, reading, and writing. These standards are aligned with English language proficiency measures. For educational settings in which Spanish is the medium of instruction, Spanish language arts standards may also serve as an anchor for instruction and assessment (State of Wisconsin, 2005).

Although there are no national or state standards for cross-cultural competence, this area of learning is an important aspect of all language education programs. Broad standards for cross-cultural competence have been developed for adults that can be adapted and used with younger students in K–12 settings. Cross-cultural competence includes three major goals, developing: (1) cross-cultural understanding, (2) intercultural communication skills, and (3) cross-cultural collaboration and problem-solving skills (Kibler & Nguyen, 2002). Cross-cultural understanding refers to the knowledge and empathy necessary to relate to people from cultural backgrounds other than one's own. Intercultural communication skills include the ability to communicate verbally and nonverbally across familiar and unfamiliar cultural settings in a variety of situations (which may or may not involve a second language). Cross-cultural collaboration and problem-solving skills enable a person to function with relative ease across cultural boundaries (not borders) to accomplish personal and mutually agreed-upon goals.

For language education programs to be viable, their learning goals should mirror learning standards and assessment. In practice, they are, in addition, likely to be personalized and reflective of the community at large, thereby moving beyond what is required at a federal or state level. In this way, state, district, program, and classroom assessments complement each other in monitoring students' progress toward achieving learning goals.

Assessment Principle 2. Decision making is based on multiple measures that include information from formative and summative assessment across levels of implementation to yield a rich array of quantitative, qualitative, and combined types of evidence.

Assessment implies the use of more than one type of measurement. In other words, multiple data sources are necessary for educational decision making. Some types of measurement, such as summative standardized, norm-referenced tests, yield purely quantitative or numerical information. Results from these assessments are expressed as scores, such as in stanines, percentiles, or normal curve equivalents. Other forms of measurement rely solely on descriptive information, such as formative writing samples from students' personal journals. Some performance-based measures offer quantitative and qualitative information. For example, students may produce original oral or writing samples (the qualitative data) and their performance may be interpreted with rubrics that use descriptive criteria, which may then be converted to a score or a proficiency level designation (a quantitative or numerical summary).

Both qualitative and quantitative information are necessary for language education programs because the learning goals of such programs are geared to student growth in affect, language, and cognitive development.. The measurement of affect—that is, students' attitudes, feelings, motivation, and interests—can be done numerically, based on responses to a checklist or rating scale. These types of measures are extremely useful in gauging the development of cross-cultural understanding and competency. These data also give more detailed, richer, personal, and authentic information about student learning overall.

Assessment data should be gathered in both quantitative and qualitive forms (as well as mixed forms). Qualitative data are generally connected with classroom,assessment; quantitative data are usually associated with district- and state-level assessments, and mixed forms of data may apply to any level—the classroom, program, district, or state. The purpose of the assessment, the importance of the decision to be made, and the time available for the assessment determine what kind of data may be appropriately collected and how the results are to be reported. A comprehensive portrait of the student as a learner can be obtained only by the systematic collection of different types of data over time.

Assessment Principle 3. Assessment at the state and district levels complements strongly supported assessment at the program and classroom levels.

Large-scale, summative assessment at the state and district levels is part of school life. Although there has been a continuous cry for improving standardized testing (Darling-Hammond, Ancess, & Falk, 1995; Shephard, 1989; Wiggins, 1993), federal legislation perpectuates high-stakes, student testing.

Based on the No Child Left Behind (NCLB) Act of 2001, the latest authorization of the Elementary and Secondary School Act, as of the 2006–07 academic year, states must be in compliance with testing requirements by having developed or adapted measures of academic achievement in reading/English-language arts and mathematics, to be administered annually in grades 3 through 8 and once in high school, as well as measures of achievement in science to be administered at benchmark grade levels. In addition, states are to have standards-based measures of English language proficiency for ELLs at grade levels K–12.

To counter the negative consequences of high-stakes state assessment, especially for ELLs, for whom most tests of academic achievement are not valid, local assessment results must be defensible. Classrooms and language education programs should develop or adopt locally relevant measures that produce reliable, valid, and meaningful data. Once these assessments are able to demonstrate a technical rigor equal to that of high-stakes tests, teachers will have clear evidence and defendable claims for valid student performance, and the data can then contribute to state and district accountability requirements.

To achieve such technical rigor, assessment at the classroom and program levels must be consistent and uniform in its content, format, delivery, and interpretation across individual students, classrooms, or grade levels. This consistency allows the establishment of a standard means of embarking on assessment and enables data from this common assessment to be more reliable and thus generalizable to language education programs and districts as a whole. For instance, a district-wide writing rubric with agreed-upon criteria and student anchor and bench-mark papers enables teachers to communicate about student performance using a shared language.

Assessment Principle 3 underscores the importance of classroom-level data as a complement to data obtained by statewide and district-wide testing. The use of local data not only contributes to explaining student performance, it lends legitimacy to the program's operation as well. The advantages of using classroom data include:

- Offering immediate, targeted feedback

- Giving diagnostic information

- Giving meaningful results

- Reflecting local program learning goals

- Being a direct outgrowth of the curriculum

- Providing information to inform instruction

- Assisting in differentiating instruction and assessment

- Promoting deep learning

Classroom assessment can be used to plan and tailor instruction for individual student needs. As stated by O'Malley and Pierce (1996), this form of assessment is authentic in that it reflects student learning, achievement, motivation, and attitudes within an instructionally relevant context. Its authenticity is recognized in the BASIC model. In sum, program and classroom measures are the solid base that teachers rely on to make ongoing decisions about their students. As contributors to the accountability equation, program and classroom data are given some weight, which is ultimately balanced against the weight of state and district assessment.

Assessment Principle 4. Students' language proficiency, as demonstrated by their growth in language development, is distinct from their academic achievement, their attainment of conceptual skills and knowledge. The assessment of language proficiency and academic achievement is unique, with each measure specifically crafted to fulfill a specific purpose.

Assessment Principle 4 addresses one of the most basic notions of assessment, construct validity. Construct validity denotes the extent to which the stated purpose is accurately measured by the assessment tool. In language education programs, that means that the documentation of language development, as exemplified in language proficiency standards, should be distinct from the documentation of content mastery outlined in academic content standards. Table 2.1 lists the specific purposes for assessing language proficiency and academic achievement. These distinct purposes must be kept in mind when planning, implementing, and evaluating language education programs. Is it fair, for example, for ELLs to have to demonstrate their mathematical acumen by trying to read symbolic text in an unfamiliar language? If the purpose of assessment is for the student to demonstrate academic achievement, language should not interfere with the measurement of knowledge and skills in a specific content area.

Language learners' demonstration of their language proficiency is measured by growth over time, starting in kindergarten. For ELLs, this longitudinal gathering of cohort data is based on annual measurement of progress in English across the language domains of listening, speaking, reading, and writing (as well as comprehension, the combination of

Table 2.1. Purposes for Assessment of Language Proficiency and Academic Achievement in Language Education Programs

Language Proficiency	*Academic Achievement*
• Contribute to the identification and placement of ELLs	• Monitor students' content knowledge and skills to inform teaching and differentiate instruction
• Monitor the progress of ELLs' English language development to inform teaching and differentiate instruction	• Ascertain if students are 'proficient' in regard to grade-level expectations or standards
• Document growth of English language development over time for state accountability	• Contribute to evaluation of the overall educational program
• Contribute to the reclassification of ELLs when deemed English language proficient	
• Contribute to the evaluation of language program services	

listening and reading). Students' mastery of content is reflected in their academic achievement, starting in third grade. According to the NCLB Act, this measurement is absolute: either students have reached the benchmark of 'proficient' or they have not.

In light of the sanctions that threaten teachers, schools, and districts, it is imperative that other data contribute to accountability, especially at the local level. Whether or not achievement data in a language other than English are collected at a state level, if instruction is delivered in a language other than English at the local level, then achievement in that language needs to be captured and counted.

For students in dual language or enrichment programs whose second language is other than English, the development of second language proficiency is an important learning goal. Ideally, measures of second language proficiency are parallel to and comparable with measures of English language proficiency. Unfortunately, such measures are scarce. Those that do exist are primarily in Spanish and are designed for native Spanish speakers; however, even these are not currently standards-based.

Because English language proficiency and academic achievement are grounded in two sets of learning standards, English language proficiency and academic content standards, it is relatively easy to maintain their separation for assessment. Those students whose second language is a language other than English are recognized through learning goals and language objectives. Figure 2.1 illustrates the interconnections among standards, assessment, curriculum, and instruction in language education programs. Curriculum and instruction, at the center of diagram, are the means by which language and content are integrated for language learners.

Assessment Principle 5. Well-articulated learning goals that stem from a program's vision and mission are formulated, shared, and supported by all constituents, including students, parents, teachers, administrators, and boards of education.

The last assessment principle, although not directly related to assessment, is perhaps the broadest and helps ground the others. It underscores the importance of having a shared vision that has been built on consensus and is subject to continuous renewal. Everyone in the language education community should be aware of the program and, to the extent feasible, should have opportunities to advocate for it. This cohesive force will help unify and solidify efforts to endorse and sustain language education.

Every language education program has three broad areas for formu-

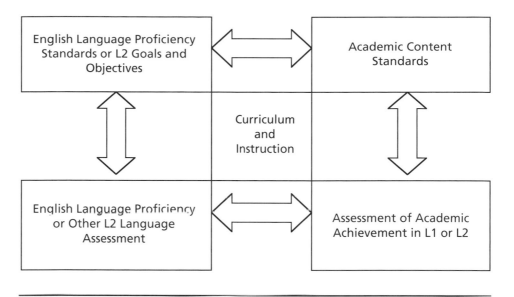

Figure 2.1 Anchors for assessment of language proficiency and academic achievement in language education programs.

lating learning goals: academic learning, language development, and cross-cultural competence. The interaction between and among these goals ultimately creates the climate that permeates the programs. Specific goals do vary; however, language education programs by definition should promote development and learning in all three areas.

For example, a language proficiency goal for dual language, immersion, or one-way developmental programs would center on students' development in two languages and promote additive bilingualism. In language education programs where the native language is used as a vehicle for acquiring English, on the other hand, the language policy would ultimately favor English, with a lessening in native language instruction, resulting in subtractive bilingualism. A similar notion applies to language instruction for academic achievement: different programs allocate the use of language in various ways across grade levels. For instance, some programs specify percent of time per language, others may use one language for introducing new concepts and another for reinforcing learning. The development and promotion of languages and cultures are an integral part of all language education programs.

These five assessment principles are the foundation on which the BASIC model has been developed. They are derived from research and theory, and define the role of assessment and the use of data in any language education program. Worksheet 2A invites readers to evaluate their current assessment practices according to these principles.

The BASIC Model

In Figure 2.2, the BASIC model is represented by concentric equilateral triangles in which a confluence of assessments, reflective of curriculum and instruction, is framed by learning standards, learning goals, and learning benchmarks that are grounded in contextual information. The base of the model is formed and informed by both program and classroom assessment, where information is gathered throughout the year. This foundation of the model is internal to the functioning of language

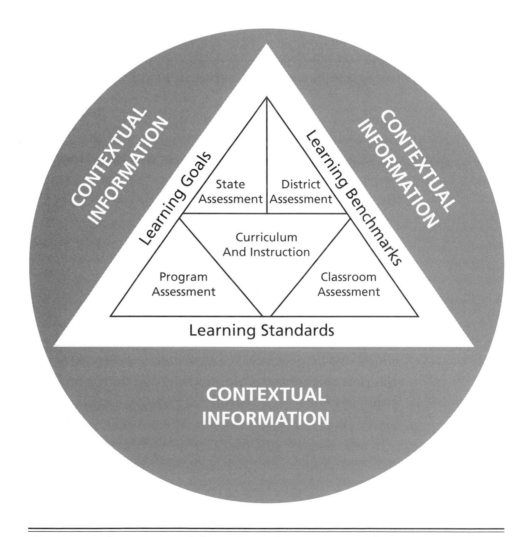

Figure 2.2 The BASIC model: a Balanced Assessment and Accountability System, Inclusive and Comprehensive.

education programs, closely tied to curriculum and instruction, and is capable of operating independently from externally imposed district or state tests, which form the apex of the triangle. Viewed in its entirety as an authentic assessment and accountability system, the model accounts for how evidence from different types of data sources are pooled and shared to inform teaching and learning. The model is readily adapted to different language education programs at the school and district levels.

Influences on the BASIC Model

In designing an assessment framework for a school district or school, program leaders and administrators must consider the context and structure of the language education program in that setting. The implementation of the BASIC model in any setting is shaped by three important influences: community and student characteristics, the mission and vision of the language education program, and the interests of the major constituents. These forces are not only critical to the development of the model, they are also vital to its maintenance, support, and advocacy. Teachers and administrators interested in implementing the BASIC model in their local school context should begin by analyzing the student population and the community climate in relation to the overall purpose of the language education program.

Community and Student Characteristics

The characteristics of the student population are a determining factor in the types of language education programs that are available to serve the community. For example, if a school district has a relatively equal distribution and concentration of minority and majority language groups within a school (e.g., of Spanish and English speakers, or of Japanese and English speakers), especially at the primary grade levels, then dual language or two-way immersion (TWI) becomes a viable option. If, however, a school district includes a heterogeneous mix of second language learners from 30 or more linguistic and cultural backgrounds, the feasibility of implementing a dual language program is remote. In this case, schools are likely to develop an ESL or ELD program. In all cases, the language education program must be cognizant of and build on the linguistic and cultural diversity of the community.

At the school level, part of the demographic information needed to formulate a strong assessment system for the language education program is the numbers and distribution of linguistically and culturally diverse students across grade levels and, within that subgroup, the determination of which ones are ELLs. By identifying these students, administrators can more readily group them for specific language services. For example, if there is a cluster of ELLs at the kindergarten level whose numbers tend to increase with each school year, then exploring the option of a one-way developmental bilingual or dual language program, where literacy is introduced in the students' first language, may be appropriate. If, on the other hand, there are newly arrived ELLs at the middle school level with limited formal schooling, an ESL or ELD program with a strong sheltered instructional component may be most effective. The program designed for a specific population of language learners in turn influences the types of assessments that need to be conducted.

Mission and Vision of the Language Education Program

Mission and vision statements guide the direction of language education programs within the greater school community and remind all those who are involved of the reasons for serving children. The mission is more global in nature, while the vision shows how the mission is realized within a specific language education program. The vision statement, crafted by constituents, helps unify the language education program to make it internally cohesive. The mission statement in particular serves as an accountability reminder to major constituents of the program regarding the beliefs and values underlying their language education program.

Interests of the Constituents

Constituents in education include parents, students, teachers, administrators, and boards of education. Every constituent's input contributes to the process of developing and refining the language education program. Their voice is important and their involvement is key to program effectiveness. Constituents are also valuable data sources and serve as a barometer of internal accountability.

The support of the community-at-large is vital to the stability of language education programs. Family and community members' participation in classrooms, on committees, and in school improvement efforts contribute to the program's visibility and vitality. Family members apprised of student performance, program highlights, and school events in their native language and English on a regular basis are more involved in their children's education.

Boards of education, as school districts' policymaking bodies, are part of the communication and accountability loop for language education programs. It is important that these decision makers have a thorough understanding of the research that underlies language education programs, the language acquisition process, and assessment results. Equipped with this knowledge, board members are better able to support administrators' and principals' decisions about the types of language education programs they implement, the hiring of highly qualified teachers, allocating physical space, and coordinating resources and services for the program.

The assessment information gathered through the implementation of the BASIC model in a particular language education program can in turn be used to influence the major constituents' decisions and attitudes, to refine the language education program's vision and goals, and to make a positive impact on the students and community-at-large. Worksheet 3 in the Appendix asks educators to consider how community and student characteristics, program mission and goals, and major constituents influence their language education program and assessment practices.

The Components of the BASIC Model

The BASIC model does not operate in isolation; it functions within language education programs in schools and in the community at large. The BASIC model itself is inclusive because it considers the classroom the central hub for data collection and the teacher a valued contributor to that effort. The model is comprehensive because it relies on different forms of data gathered at specified intervals to yield a portrait, rather than a snapshot, of student learning. Finally, it is a system, because there is a deliberate and agreed-upon convergence of thinking on the part of educators in how data inform teaching and learning while simultaneously helping to gauge program effectiveness.

This section describes the components of the BASIC model, starting from the outside, with contextual information, and working across the sides of the outer triangle in Figure 2.2: learning goals, standards, and benchmarks. We then move into its core, curriculum and instruction, and discuss purposes for and types of assessments used across four levels of implementation: state, district, program, and classroom.

Contextual Information

Contextual information serves multiple purposes. For example, it provides the background for implementing language education programs, it is a validity check to ensure programs are operating according to plan, and it drives internal decision making so that the program is responsive to local needs. Contextual information thus grounds the BASIC model within the local setting. Knowing the context in which language education programs are implemented makes the data generated by the programs real, appropriate, and meaningful.

Historical data are the primary sources of background information about students. Information regarding students' continuity of education and literacy practices helps in their initial placement and is instrumental in determining what is expected of individual students. The education of highly mobile students who have had interrupted schooling differs from the education of those who have had a continuous schooling experience. It is reasonable to expect that students who do not have a firm foundation in the native language or who have not developed a strong literacy base are not likely to acquire English literacy at the same pace as those with highly developed literacy skills.

Some historical data collection is quite regulated, being largely bound to and guided by state, district, or programmatic policy; an example is the Home Language Survey. Data collected on students at initial entry into a school or school district describing their demographics and prior educational experiences provide insight into their membership in a classroom community. Other historical data can be gathered by teachers within the classroom. For example, information on students' exposure to, use of, and preferences for languages inside and outside of school is useful in planning instruction (Gottlieb, 2006).

Another important piece of historical information that allows teachers insight into their students is the continuity of services. ELLs who receive pre-K instruction in English when their native language is not fully developed and who then qualify for bilingual services in kindergarten, only to be switched back to English-only instruction in first grade, often appear to have learning disabilities. However, their struggle is often attributable to the inconsistent language support services they have received. Conversely, ELLs in well-designed language education programs where there is clear articulation between grade levels fare better. Thus, historical data provide the context in which language education programs can best serve the students.

Contextual information is useful in shaping language education programs, validating their worth, and it also informs decisions internal to the programs themselves. With historical data, instruction and assessment can be differentiated with a deeper understanding of student performance. In essence, the BASIC model, although representative of language education programs that are grounded in the local community, function within the greater context of schooling.

Learning Goals, Standards, and Benchmarks

Moving to the outer triangle in Figure 2.2, we find learning goals, standards, and benchmarks, which define the foci for curriculum, instruction, and assessment. Together, they frame the BASIC model and are integral to its operation. This learning frame, when solidly established, helps drive the quality of the BASIC model. Learning goals are broad areas of commitment, built from consensus on the part of educators and the community-at-large, for language education programs.

On the left side of the triangle we have positioned learning goals. There are generally three broad learning goals that guide language education programs: language development, academic learning, and cross-cultural competence. All programs for ELLs, whether they are bilingual or English-only programs, expect ELLs to achieve academically in English, develop English language proficiency, and become culturally competent in U.S. society. Dual language programs have the additional goals of bilingualism, biliteracy, academic achievement in two languages, and positive cultural understanding and intercultural communication competence for their target populations. All educators who work in the language education program must be clear about their goals for their target populations.

At the base of the triangle are learning standards that serve as the foundation for assessment, curriculum, and instruction. Learning standards have become incorporated into school life as national organizations and federal legislation have made standards-based reform an integral part of the educational landscape. The Elementary and Secondary School Act of 1994, known as the Improving America's Schools Act, required states to develop academic content standards. With the most recent reauthorization of this legislation, in the form of the NCLB Act of 2001, learning standards have been expanded to include English language proficiency for ELLs. States have all developed English language proficiency standards, either independently or in consortia (an example is the World-Class Instructional Design and Assessment or WIDA Consortium), and Teachers of English to Speakers of Other Languages (TESOL) recently issued national English language proficiency standards.

Accountability extends to a dual set of standards for ELLs. English language proficiency standards define the social and academic language along developmental continua that is requisite for accessing, processing, and understanding content. Academic content standards delineate the knowledge and skills of grade-level subject matter (Gottlieb, 2006). In addition, although not required, a handful of states and the WIDA Consortium have developed Spanish language arts standards to guide teachers who use Spanish as the medium of assessment and instruction in language education programs. The American Council of Teachers of Foreign Languages (ACTFL) introduced national standards for foreign language education in 1995. When a language education program has instruction in a language for which there are no national or state standards, such as Japanese in a dual language setting, schools or districts must take on the task of developing local standards.

On the right side of the triangle are learning benchmarks. Learning benchmarks are related to learning standards in that they specify the expectations of students at different points in time. At the state level, benchmarks are expressed as grade-level expectations, sometimes represented as the standards themselves, sometimes independently (as in the Northeast Compact), and at times posed within state assessment frameworks. Often these learning benchmarks are adopted by school districts which view student performance relative to meeting state standards.

For language education programs, learning benchmarks must be established for two languages, as in dual language settings, or adjusted based on historical information on the students. Learning benchmarks for students in a newcomers center who arrive with limited literacy or academic skills in their first language may differ substantially from learning benchmarks for students in gifted language classes. Native English speakers most likely will not have the same learning benchmarks for their second language as ELLs have for acquiring English as their second language.

In classrooms, teachers use learning benchmarks as progress markers to monitor student growth along a developmental pathway toward reaching standards or grade-level expectations. When the progress markers are clearly identified, they guide the design of appropriate assessment and instructional practices. In this way the learning standards, goals, and benchmarks frame the core components of the BASIC model: assessment, curriculum, instruction.

Table 2.2 lists the components of the BASIC model that inform assessment, curriculum, and instructional activities. The table includes examples of sources of contextual information that ground the BASIC model and specifies the learning standards, goals, and benchmarks that frame the model. Worksheet 4 asks educators to describe how the components of the BASIC model ground and frame their language education program and assessment practices.

Having explored the dimensions of the outer triangle, we now focus our attention on the core of the BASIC model. Here we see assessment at different levels of implementation—state, district, program, or classroom—having an impact on curriculum and instruction. The strength of the model is the balance that is created by having program and classroom assessment along the base for internal accountability purposes. This foundation acts as a counterbalance to state and district assessment at the top of the triangle, which represent external accountability demands.

Table 2.2 Components of the BASIC Model that Influence Assessment, Curriculum, and Instruction

Contextual Information	Learning Goals	Learning Standards	Learning Benchmarks
• Home language surveys • Other surveys (e.g., family, student, community) • Historical data	• Cross-cultural competence • Language development • Academic learning	• English language proficiency standards • Academic content standards, including Spanish language arts standards	• Grade-level expectations • Growth markers along developmental continua

Curriculum and Instruction

Curriculum and instruction, positioned at the core of the BASIC model, are informed by assessment from all angles. A wide spectrum of assessments provides a comprehensive picture of what students know and can do, and allows teachers to differentiate instructional strategies accordingly (Gregory & Kuzmich, 2004). The data generated from assessment connect learning goals, learning standards (and their performance indicators), and learning benchmarks to classroom instruction in language education programs.

A standards-driven curriculum with rich, stimulating content provides enhanced opportunities to students. When standards are shared with students and parents, the curriculum becomes more transparent and viable. Core elements of standards-based learning are beneficial to all students but are especially advantageous to ELLs because they include the following:

- Authentic learning tasks

- Connection of instruction to students' lives and experiences

- Deeper examination of student work

- Increased focus on language and literacy development within content-centered learning (Lachat, 2004)

Instruction in today's world is guided by information from assessment, which in turn is grounded in learning standards. English language proficiency standards, by being anchored in academic content standards and descriptive of the language development process, are a natural venue for generating ideas for curriculum, instruction, and assessment at the classroom or district level (Gottlieb, 2006; Gottlieb, Carnuccio, Ernst-Slavit, & Katz, 2006). Differentiated instructional strategies for ELLs according to both their language proficiency levels and conceptual understanding can then focus on the unique needs of the students while supporting both language and academic learning.

Assessment

The BASIC model is not a hierarchical model because authentic assessment and accountability operate on various levels simultaneously. However, it does recognize the hierarchical nature of implementing educational policies and procedures (from states to districts to programs to classrooms) and the constraints imposed from one level to the next. We do not include the national level in our model, as federal mandates are universal for all states, but choose instead to highlight assessment for those levels of implementation in which constituents have a voice and can make a difference.

There are two major purposes for assessment, which are commonly referred to as formative and summative. Formative assessment is used to gauge students' progress and growth as they learn and to provide information to guide daily instructional decisions. Summative assessment is used to measure students' proficiency or achievement as a result of learning. This discussion begins by describing the overall purposes for assessment, followed by a presentation of three types of assessment. We conclude by identifying how different types of assessment are used for different purposes at each of the classroom, program, district, and state levels of implementation.

Assessment for Learning   Formative assessment entails the collection, analysis, and use of data on a regular basis that directly informs and helps to further shape teaching and learning. It generally takes place at the classroom, program, and district levels. Stiggins (2002) coined the phrase "assessment *for* learning" to describe formative classroom assessment strategies that inform instruction and motivate students to learn. Successful assessment for learning requires accuracy of assessment and the effective use of assessment data to enhance learning. According to Stiggins, Arter, Chapuis, and Chapuis (2004), formative assessment on the classroom level is effective when:

- Assessment is aligned to individual student learning targets with clear purposes.

- Assessment is designed to reflect student performances and provides credible information about student learning and achievement.

- Assessment results are communicated effectively with students in a timely manner to guide learning.

- Assessment that provides both descriptive and evaluative feedback is used to encourage students to take the next step in their learning.

- Assessment engages students in self reflection and involves students in making their own learning decisions (Chappuis, 2004).

Effective classroom assessment practices use multiple sources of information, are integrated into the learning and teaching routines in the classroom, and entail collaboration between students and educators.

Actually, formative assessment represents a continuum of measures. Formative assessment can be idiosyncratic to individual teachers at the classroom level, where information is student-specific. On the one hand, it can be based on spontaneous observation leading to or emanating from a teachable moment, during which information about a student is processed quickly and feedback is given almost instantaneously. On the other hand, some formative measures are planned, such as the collection of anecdotal information on specific behaviors of groups of students at designated intervals. If the measures are performance-based—for example, if students are actively engaged in producing work samples—then student work may be interpreted through a uniform set of criteria or rubrics. At the other end of the continuum, formative assessment may involve multiple classes, as a grade level, or even across the entire language education program; those common assessments are more standard in their administration and interpretation.

The range of formative assessment is shown in Table 2.3. As is evident, the use of information from formative assessment varies by level of implementation. Worksheet 5 asks educators to review the range of formative assessments used in their settings across the classroom, program, and district levels of implementation, and to identify the primary uses of formative assessment.

Assessment of Learning   Summative assessment is used to measure students' achievement and proficiency as a result of learning; in essence, it is intended to be a summary of student performance at a particular point in time after a specified period of learning. Following Stiggins (2006a), we use the term "assessment of learning" to describe this purpose for assessment.

Some summative measures in language education programs are mandated by the state or district, such as the large-scale tests administered annually to ELLs on both their English language proficiency and academic achievement. However, this information is not sufficient for dual language or one-way developmental bilingual programs that expect students to become bilingual and biliterate. For these students, summa-

Table 2.3   The Range of Formative Assessments

Parameter	Level of Implementation		
	District	*Program*	*Classroom*
Purpose of measures	Status of students relative to learning benchmarks	Overall progress and growth of groups of students over time in the program	Individual student progress and growth
Students assessed	All	Those in a program	Individual or subgroups
Types of data	Quantitative and qualitative	Quantitative and qualitative	Qualitative and quantitative
Use of data	Improve district services	Improve program services	Improve teaching and learning

tive measures in languages other than English (usually Spanish) administered at the program level are of equal importance and value.

It is important to recognize that formative data collected over time can also provide summative information about student achievement and proficiency at designated times, such as a marking period. However, summative data are generally collected at only one point in time, such as with large-scale testing.

Types of Assessment: Idiosyncratic, Standard, and Standardized   In the BASIC model, formative and summative uses of information can be further categorized into three types of assessment: idiosyncratic, standard, and standardized measures.

Assessment that is idiosyncratic is personalized for individual teachers, and the data are used to facilitate student learning and improve the internal functioning of the classroom or the language education program. With idiosyncratic assessment, teachers are able to give immediate feedback to students. Similarly, coordinators or directors of language education programs can quickly inform teachers.

Teachers gain a wealth of information about their students on an informal basis, through observations of everyday interaction in the context of the classroom. Teachers are constantly giving verbal responses to students and making on-the-spot adjustments to their lessons based on observation or "kid watching." They react instantaneously to their students' breakthrough moments as well as moments of confusion. Such informal data are the most sensitive and variable, as they reflect the individual teacher's perceptions of student behavior. Yet this information is extremely valuable, because teachers have an intimate knowledge of their students.

Besides observation, teachers may maintain anecdotal records on individual student's behaviors, give quizzes and tests, and have their students engage in projects. Students themselves are represented in idiosyncratic assessment through self-reflection, which may be incorporated into process writing, interactive journals or learning logs, or performance-based tasks. Teachers' idiosyncratic assessment of their students' performance is at the heart of assessment for learning at the classroom level.

The second type of assessment is standard assessment. Standard assessment is administered to all students in a classroom, language education program, district, or state. It is uniform in its implementation, interpretation, and reporting of results, and can provide reliable and valid evidence of student performance. At the state level, standard assessment may consist of several performance items on statewide tests, such as writing in response to reading or constructed response math items. At the district level, students may be required to produce writing samples from a uniform prompt, which are then scored by a district-wide rubric, or they may have their reading monitored through informal reading inventories. At the program level, standard assessment may consist of an observation matrix for L1 and L2 or required entries in students' portfolios. At the classroom level, teachers at one grade level may collaborate in designing a common thematic unit of instruction in which they embed common performance-based assessments using identical tasks. These common assessments, collaboratively designed and implemented by teachers, are at the heart of assessment for learning at the program level.

Standard assessment is a viable component of an authentic accountability system and the BASIC model. Both formative and summative assessment may be considered standard, depending on the circumstances of data collection and interpretation. Being standards-driven and reflective of curriculum and instruction, the results of standard assessments are meaningful for educators across the designated level of implementation.

The third type of assessment is standardized assessment. Standardized measures are large-scale and are administered across classrooms under the same set of conditions. They usually take the form of high-stakes testing, with consequences attached to student performance. The results of standardized tests that rank students according the population on which the tests have been normed are norm-referenced. Results that are cast in relation to specific criteria, as in learning standards, are criterion-referenced.

Standardized tests are designed to measure a broad band of competencies, whether in individual content areas or in language proficiency. The advantages to using standardized tools include producing reliable, easily scored data, providing a national perspective, and being free of the confounding effects of individual teachers (Gottlieb, 2006). They are thus applicable (and scores can be aggregated) across classroom, program, and district levels of implementation.

With some sense of the complexity of assessment and the need to have multiple forms of assessment to make informed decisions, we now turn to describing the levels of implementation for assessment within the BASIC model.

Levels of Implementation for Assessment: State, District, Program, Classroom   As components of the BASIC model, its levels of implementation are represented by the angles of the triangle in Figure 2.2. State and district assessment form the apex because they share many characteristics, the most important of which is the use of data for external accountability purposes. At the same time, there are also some distinctions, such as the use of formative information at the district level, which produces the vertical division between state and district assessment in the diagram. Program and classroom assessment occupy the two base angles of the triangle in Figure 2.2.

State and district assessment are generally outside the control of teachers, although they feel the impact of the data generated from these instruments. Program and classroom assessment counteract the effects of these externally imposed measures and bring levity, balance, and authenticity to the BASIC model. Each level of implementation contributes valuable information from assessment to yield a comprehensive and inclusive picture of student performance in language education programs. This section briefly describes these levels of implementation for assessment.

State assessment is summative and occurs within a designated window each year. ELLs are subject to testing both for English language proficiency and for academic achievement. Presently, results from state assessment are used to meet compliance with federal accountability requirements; English language proficiency tests yield data for Annual Measurable Achievement Objectives (AMAOs), while that from achievement measures determine Adequate Yearly Progress (AYP). State assessment is to be aligned with and representative of its learning standards; results, therefore, should be standards-referenced.

High-stakes tests, by their very nature, are limited in their ability to explain individual student performance. District-level assessment may utilize standardized formative measures that closely resemble high-stakes tests in that they replicate summative state efforts. In this case, formative assessment comes to take on a narrow meaning, as in benchmarking, where, in essence, mini summative assessments are administered at regular intervals, such as on a quarterly basis (Stiggins & Chappuis, 2006). Measures of Academic Progress (MAP), or other curriculum-based assessment, are examples of these types of measures.

District assessment may reflect a representative sample of learning standards, outside of those expressed in standardized measures at the state level, that exceed federal requirements. Such is the case in district writing programs where a single writing rubric (e.g., a six-trait analytic scale) is adopted. Teachers often embed this type of assessment into instruction (as in writing workshops) while simultaneously using it as a standard formative tool, district-wide, several times a year. Another example of a district assessment, especially at the primary grade level, is an informal reading inventory. Standard measures, given to individual or subgroups of students to glean information on their skills and abilities, are designed to pinpoint specific areas of strength and weakness. The results from these assessments are often used to guide differentiated classroom instruction and prescribe appropriate interventions.

As in layers of an onion we peal away, program-level assessment in the BASIC model reveals information unique to language education. That is, in dual language or one-way developmental bilingual education programs in which a language other than English is the medium of instruction, use of the other language must be mirrored in assessment. To that extent, language education programs may select standardized summative tests (if Spanish is the first language) of academic achievement on an annual or biannual basis and standard formative tools in native language reading and/or writing, given semiannually, in any language. It is incumbent upon language education programs to have reliable, valid, and relevant tools in order to accumulate defensible data and evidence to convince skeptical constituents and reassure others that learning goals are being met. When commercially made tools are not available, as is frequently the case for the less commonly taught languages, practitioners can collaborate within and across programs and districts to develop common program assessments of language development (see Chapter 4).

In addition, districts may choose to have an accurate, standard barometer of ELLs' progress or status in English language proficiency that is differentiated through leveled readers, such as the ELL Assessment Kit (Gottlieb, 2007). Assessment conducted at multiple points in a school year within various contexts and purposes can be more diagnostic and descriptive of student growth and achievement (Afflerbach, 2005). Information from program assessment has a more direct impact on curricular and instructional decisions than that from state or district measures.

The classroom is the centerpiece for gathering evidence on student performance and program effectiveness. Although often neglected in statewide accountability, the classroom is a tremendously important contributor to an internal, authentic assessment and accountability system. Assessment experts have long advocated for the important role of classroom assessment in teaching and learning (Ainsworth & Viegut, 2006; Darling-Hammond, Ancess, & Falk, 2005; O'Malley & Pierce,

Table 2.4 Examples of Assessments Used at Each Level of Implementation

State Assessment	District Assessment	Program Assessment	Classroom Assessment
English language proficiency test	Tests of academic achievement in L2	Tests of academic achievement in L1	Anecdotal records
Tests of academic achievement in L2	Writing samples and rubrics in L2	Writing samples and rubrics in L1	Teacher observation
	Informal reading inventories	Observation matrix in L1 and L2	Unit tests and quizzes
	Reading rubrics		Performance assessment and rubrics
			Student self-assessment

Table 2.5 Purposes and Types of Assessment at Each Level of Implementation

Level of Implementation for Assessment	Overall Purpose of Assessment	Type of Assessment*		
		Idiosyncratic	Standard	Standardized
State	Formative			
	Summative		X	X
District	Formative		X	X
	Summative		X	X
Program	Formative		X	
	Summative		X	X
Classroom	Formative	X	X	
	Summative	X	X	

*Assessment is generally not applicable to shaded cells.

1996; Popham, 2003; Shephard, 2000). Black, Harrison, Lee, Marshall, and Williams (2004) in a review of more than 675 articles provide quantitative evidence that innovations in formative classroom assessment can lead to improvements in student learning.

Broad, in-depth knowledge can be demonstrated through formative assessment (assessment for learning), not summative assessment (assessment of learning). These measures, generally reflective of learning goals, may include rubrics that are embedded within performance-based instruction (Gottlieb, 1999). For oral language development, teachers may rely on an observation matrix; for process writing, perhaps teachers have been trained on a specific holistic or analytic scale to be used with samples of student work. Students themselves can offer personal insights into the processes and products of learning through self-assessment, as evidenced in journal writing or checklists (Gottlieb, 2006).

Table 2.4 lists the kinds of assessments that are used to monitor academic learning and language proficiency development at each level of implementation. Worksheet 6 asks educators to identify the assessments they use to monitor academic learning and language development at the state, district, program, and classroom levels of implementation in their contexts.

Table 2.6 Summary of Assessments Used in the BASIC Model

	Levels of Implementation for Assessment			
	Classroom	*Program*	*District*	*State*
Purpose for measurement and use of information	Formative and summative	Formative and summative	Formative and summative	Summative
Type of assessment	Idiosyncratic within individual classrooms	Standardized and standard within language education programs	Standardized and standard across the district	Standardized and standard across the state
Frequency of data collection	Spontaneous to planned	Quarterly, monthly, and on an as needed basis	On a predetermined, scheduled schedule	Annually
Primary audience	Parents, students, teachers	Parents, students, teachers, program administrators	Program and district administrators, teachers, boards of education, greater community	Program and district administrators; boards of education, greater community

Not all types of assessment appear at each level of implementation. For example, idiosyncratic assessment is unique to programs and classrooms, while standardized assessment is affiliated with districts and states. Table 2.5 lists the purposes for and types of assessment used at state, district, program, and classroom levels of implementation. Worksheet 7 asks educators to categorize the assessments used in their language education program by type and purpose across the different levels of implementation.

Table 2.6 summarizes the characteristics of assessment used in the BASIC model at each level of implementation. Here we see the full range of purposes, types, and frequency of data collection, and the audiences most affected by the results. Depending on the language education programs as well as on district and state policies, assessment information may be gathered in English only or in both the students' native language and English.

Formative and summative assessments both contribute to an authentic accountability system. By promoting the combined use of idiosyncratic, standard, and standardized data for decision making, we gain a richer, deeper, and more meaningful account of student performance. The comprehensiveness and inclusiveness of this approach is exemplified in the BASIC model.

Distinguishing Features of the BASIC Model

The strength of the BASIC model lies in the fact that it draws heavily from the classroom and honors teachers in the process, reflects the learning goals of language education programs, integrates district requirements, and complies with state and federal mandates. The BASIC model is:

- Data-driven, relying on multiple sources and types of information collected throughout the school year

- Built on consensus and collaboration among teachers and administrators

- Balanced in its representation of classroom, district, program, and state needs and requirements

- Dynamic, evolving over time, which makes it powerful and robust

- Contextualized, using historical and programmatic information to frame evidence-based decision making

- Valid, stemming from the alignment of its components with learning goals, learning benchmarks, and learning standards

The BASIC model is built from principles of assessment for language education programs, and it is predicated on assessment and evaluation frameworks designed for language education programs (see Chapters 3 and 7 for a complete description). These frameworks guide educators in planning student assessment and explaining how the information gathered applies to improving teaching and learning.

Questions for Reflection and Action

1. Reread the five assessment principles that were presented at the beginning of the chapter. Which one is most useful to you? Why? How might you paraphrase and explain it to your colleagues?

2. Review the components of the BASIC model. How might they apply to your setting or language education program?

3. Consider the context for curriculum, instruction, and assessment in your school, district, or language education program. How might it be interpreted by different constituents (e.g., language teachers, content teachers, administrators) and what steps might you take in order for the educational community to reach a common understanding?

Developing a Comprehensive Assessment Framework for Language Education Programs

Chapter Overview

The chapter highlights the organization of curriculum and the delivery of instruction as a backdrop to the design of a comprehensive assessment framework. We guide teachers and administrators through the phases of establishing a global framework for assessment, determining the specifics of their plan, implementing the plan, and reviewing and revising the plan. This multiphase process enables educators to systematically infuse appropriate assessments into their language education programs.

Guiding Questions

- Which aspects of curriculum and instruction in your language education programs are reflected in your assessment practices?
- What kinds of formative and summative data within your language education program do you find useful?
- What might be some ways to collaborate with teachers and administrators in the design of an assessment action plan?

Key Concepts

- In standards-based education, assessment drives curriculum and instruction.
- A comprehensive assessment framework allows for multiple forms of evidence to be accrued over time.
- Multiple constituents and perspectives are integral to formulating and implementing assessment plans.

The BASIC model balances formative and summative assessment in order to produce varied data for decision making within language education programs at the classroom, program, district, and state levels of implementation. Grounded in contextual information and framed by learning goals, standards, and benchmarks, these complementary data sources offer teachers powerful tools to measure student performance throughout the school year. Implementation of the model calls for extensive planning and the development of an assessment framework that delineates the process of data collection, analysis, and reporting.

This chapter takes up the critical question, how do we build a comprehensive assessment framework for language education programs and turn it into a plan of action? We outline steps that take teachers and administrators from the conceptual to the operational phase of development. Referring to the BASIC model, we first identify the factors that affect assessment design and administration. We then provide a detailed description of how to formulate and implement authentic assessment plans for language education programs in school districts.

Defining the Parameters of Assessment Frameworks

An assessment framework that specifies what, how, when, for whom, and in which language data are collected does not function independently; it is one component of a language education program and integral to the BASIC model. Before embarking on developing an assessment framework for their language education program, however, administrators, working closely with teachers and perhaps parents, need to contemplate the program's features that help shape its organizational structure. These features include broad categories within the area of curriculum and instruction—as in the relative use of languages, the integration of language and content, the duration and continuity of services, and the rigor of teaching and learning—shown by bullets inside the triangle in Figure 3.1. As discussed in Chapter 2, these broad categories of curriculum and instruction in language education programs are (1) influenced by community and student characteristics, major constituents, and the language education program mission and vision, (2) grounded in contextual information, and (3) framed by learning goals, learning standards, and learning benchmarks. These categories are the starting point in the establishment of an assessment framework.

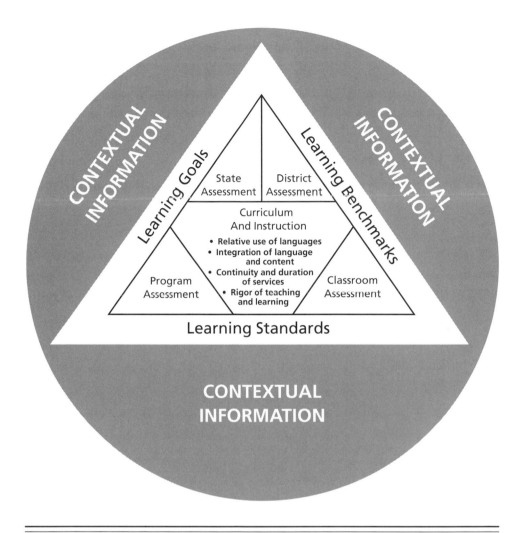

Figure 3.1 Focus on curriculum and instruction in the BASIC model.

The first category in the area of curriculum and instruction is the relative use of languages. The majority of language education programs entail varying amounts of instruction in two languages. For example, dual language programs may begin with a proportion of a language other than English for at least 50% and as much as 90% of the time, gradually diminishing over the years until a 50/50 balance of L1 and L2 is reached. At the other extreme are English-only programs, in which English language learners (ELLs) are only occasionally exposed to their native language, if at all, with instruction being delivered almost exclusively in English. In English-only programs, the decision has to focus on the amount of time spent in a sheltered English environment versus a mainstream setting. Thus, the allocation of language is a critical variable to consider in planning both assessment and instruction; in fact, it can be argued that it is the primary consideration in any *language* education program (Hilliard, 2005).

The second category to consider in our discussion of curriculum and instruction is the integration of language and content. Effective language education programs interweave language with content; that is, language is acquired by students through content area concepts (Echevarria, Vogt, & Short, 2004; Snow & Brinton, 1997). With language and content being partnered, students (and teachers) can more readily make connections between language proficiency and academic achievement. This integrated approach considers both language and content as tools for student success, and the interaction of the two allows for rich, meaningful student learning.

The third category in the area of curriculum and instruction is the duration and continuity of services. Ultimately, students maximize their attainment of language proficiency and academic achievement when sustained and directed language education programs are in place. Articulation among teachers from year to year, along with alignment of standards, assessment, curriculum, and instruction, helps ensure that students are provided with uninterrupted services as well as opportunities to scaffold learning. Only then can systematic documentation of student progress, such as in the bilingual individual instructional plan presented in Chapter 1 and discussed in Chapter 6, provide longitudinal information on student learning.

The last category that we consider in our discussion of curriculum and instruction is the rigor of teaching and learning. Students are to engage in learning, representative of a strong curriculum, where, given ample support and guidance, they are constantly challenged to succeed at their next higher level of performance (Vygotsky, 1978). Their exposure to rigorous content begins with a selection of interrelated standards that form "big ideas," coupled with ample opportunities and ways to demonstrate their proficiency. For students in language education programs, especially ELLs, instruction must take into account their unique characteristics and be crafted to support learning. Collaboration and coordination of effort among teachers is key to curriculum development, delivery of instruction, and maintenance of rigor throughout the program.

These features of curriculum and instruction, along with assessment, constitute the core of language education programs. Table 3.1 presents

Table 3.1 Implementing Curriculum and Instruction in Language Education Programs

Features of Curriculum and Instruction in Language Education Programs

Relative Use of Languages

- A clearly articulated plan for language allocation by grade level for each language group has the following features:
  - A theoretical and practical rationale
  - An outline of language use by content area
  - The amount of time per day or week for each language by language group
  - The language of assessment reflective of the language of instruction.
- Teachers self-monitor and adhere to the plan.

Integration of Language and Content

- Thematic units of instruction tie language proficiency and academic content standards and provide for:
  - Language and content objectives in lesson planning
  - Ample supports for students (visual, graphic, interactive) for both language and cognitive development
  - Differentiated instruction for both language and content
  - Independent assessment

Continuity and Duration of Services

- The language education program functions within a school's or district's general education program and provides for:
  - A logical and realistic plan for students' progression of language development over multiple years
  - Coordination of services
  - Continuity of language education services
  - Teacher involvement in sustained professional development to ensure ongoing articulation
  - Documentation of students' language development and academic achievement from year to year.
- Parents are involved in and informed about the language education program.

The Rigor of Teaching and Learning

- Teachers jointly plan for assessment, curriculum, and instruction. This collaborative planning includes:
  - Thoughtful deliberation in the selection of standards
  - Consideration of students' educational backgrounds
  - Use of students' linguistic and cultural diversity as a resource
  - Providing accessible, engaging, hands-on learning opportunities
  - Providing scaffolded instruction through interrelated activities and tasks
- Students are given continuous feedback on their performance.

examples of these features by the categories identified in Figure 3.1. Worksheet 8 asks educators to consider to what degree they explicitly address these features of curriculum and instruction in their language education program.

The BASIC model for standards-based education in language education programs, shown in Figure 3.1, is the starting point for envisioning the building of assessment frameworks. Thinking about standards-based curriculum and instruction within program delivery allows administrators and teachers to envision how assessment is to be interwoven. The specifics of this process begin with the overall design for assessment.

Designing an Assessment Plan

Student assessment, anchored in standards, is directly related to accountability. In language education programs, assessment must embrace all goals, including students' development of cross-cultural competence and second language proficiency. Each goal needs to be aligned with the standards (state standards in the case of academic achievement and English language proficiency, and more general standards in the case of cross-cultural competence). Each goal must have explicit measurable objectives that are incorporated into assessment, curriculum, and instruction.

The development of either a single assessment framework that evolves over time or a series of related frameworks may be conceptualized as a four-phase process, moving from a generalized framework to an operational plan. The product of each phase, its use, and the audience are outlined in Table 3.2, followed by a brief description.

Phase 1: Establishing a Global Framework for Assessment

An overall assessment framework that exemplifies the BASIC model is outlined in Table 3.3 and serves as a template for subsequent phases. This plan delineates the elements to be contemplated in the design and implementation of language education programs. Taken together, the assessment framework and plan yield an inclusive and comprehensive view of data-driven outcomes reflective of the assessment principles presented in Chapter 2.

Language educators begin with the three goals of all language educa-

Table 3.2 Phases of Development of an Assessment Plan

	Product	*Use and Audience*
Phase 1	Establish a global framework for assessment	• Organizational tool for teachers and administrators for assessment and instructional design • Means to monitor student progress in all core areas of learning
Phase 2	Identify and balance the selection of specific assessment measures, according to various purposes, stipulated in the framework	• Topics for professional development of various constituents • Management tool for directors and coordinators of language education programs
Phase 3	Develop and implement a specific assessment plan with a time frame and timeline for conducting assessments	• Time for piloting, adjusting and institutionalizing each assessment practice • Implementation guide and support for teachers and administrators throughout the school year
Phase 4	Review, update, and improve the plan	• Flexible assessment system that is practical, useful, and defensible

tion programs: cross-cultural communication, second language development, and academic learning. These program goals must be aligned with their respective standards, which serve as guideposts that anchor all aspects of the program. The purposes of assessment (assessment for learning and assessment of learning) relative to the program goals dictate the types of assessment measures that are selected or developed. Assessment proceeds at the classroom, program, district, and state levels through systematic collection of information about the students' L1 and L2, the languages used in the language education program. That which is formative, in large part, yields qualitative results, while large-scale measures at the district and state levels provide the quantitative dimension. Finally, the combination of types of evidence, or the qualitative and quantitative data sources, paves the way to rich, descriptive information on student performance on both a formative and summative basis.

This introductory phase stimulates initial discussion between teachers and administrators and serves as the starting point for collaboration.

Table 3.3 A Global Assessment Framework for Language Education Programs

	Cross-cultural competence standards	Language proficiency standards	Academic content standards
Program goals	Cross-cultural competence	Language development	Academic learning
Purposes for assessment	Formative and summative	Formative and summative	Formative and summative
Languages of assessment	L1 and L2	L2	L1 and L2
Evidence	Qualitative and quantitative	Qualitative and quantitative	Qualitative and quantitative

Because the entire process is built on consensus among educators, it is important to establish communication links from the onset. In this way teachers are aware, very early on, that their voice in decision making is heard. The language education program coordinators encourage teachers to share ways in which to monitor student progress within the instructional cycle that is an outgrowth of standards, program goals, and diverse forms of data collection. The result is a well-articulated framework or a series of frameworks that anchors an overall assessment plan.

Phase 2: Determining the Specifics of a Plan

Once a global framework is established, the next step is to list the goals of the language education program and identify specific assessment measures, the languages of administration, and the types of data to be generated. In this second phase, a broad spectrum of assessments is matched to components within the language education program to ensure ample coverage of learning standards and goals. For instance, for language proficiency, provision must be made for assessing each language domain—listening, speaking, reading, and writing. Likewise, for academic achievement, information is to be gathered from each major content area—language arts, mathematics, science, and social studies.

The selection of the language(s) of assessments is an important consideration in the design of the assessment framework. Table 3.4 presents

Table 3.4 Example of a Framework for a 50/50 Spanish-English Dual-Language Program with Specific Assessment Measures

Parameter	Learning Goals, Standards, and Benchmarks		
	Cross-cultural Competence	*Second Language Development*	*Academic Learning*
Areas of assessment	• Cross-cultural understanding • Intercultural communication • Cross-cultural problem-solving and collaboration	• Listening • Speaking • Reading • Writing	• Language Arts • Math • Science • Social Studies
Language(s) of assessment	L1 and L2	L2	L1 and L2
Formative assessments	• Observation with notes or checklists • Student interviews • Student self-assessment • Interactive journals • Surveys (e.g., attitudes, friendship patterns) • Sociograms	• Locally developed L2 learning checklist • Language observation matrices • Informal interviews • Story retelling • Informal reading inventories • Reading/writing rubrics • Reading responses/ logs • Anecdotal observation notes • Student self-assessment • Curriculum-based assessment	• Interactive journals • Learning logs • Performance-based work samples • Criterion-referenced achievment tests • Anecdotal observation notes • Student self-assessment • Curriculum-based assessment
Summative assessments	• Cultural competence questionnaire	• Standardized language proficiency measures • Locally developed L2 learning checklist • End of unit quiz or test	• Performance-based work samples • End of unit quizzes or tests • Achievement tests

a sample assessment framework from School District 54 for a 50/50 dual language program with two distinct languages groups: the L2 for ELLs is English, while for proficient English students, it is Spanish.

Of course, the assessment frameworks developed for particular language education programs will differ. There is variability in the amount of assessment and instruction in L1 and L2, depending on the type of language education program and the grade level of the students. For example, in monolingual settings it is assumed that English is the sole language utilized, whereas in kindergarten classrooms in dual language contexts assessment and instruction may occur in a language other than English up to 90% of the time. Frameworks and plans are to be adjusted according to the specific characteristics of each educational setting. As mutually agreed upon by teachers, the choice of the language(s) of assessment should reflect the extent to which each language is used for instruction.

At the program level, the alignment of program goals, languages of instruction, and areas of assessment with their associated classroom and district or state measures becomes transparent. Therefore, the assessment plan must take into consideration the relative importance of each learning goal: cross-cultural competence, language development, and academic learning. The selection of assessment measures and methods is based not only on the availability of assessments but also on how much weight a particular assessment carries in the overall assessment and accountability plan. In addition, assessment tools at the classroom level must be used to counterbalance the district's and state's standardized instruments.

As discussed in Chapter 2, there are two major purposes for assessment: assessment for learning, or formative assessment, and assessment of learning, or summative assessment. Although formative assessment data acquired over time can be used for summative purposes at a moment in time, such as at the end of a marking period, specific assessment measures tend to lend themselves to either formative or summative purposes. In Table 3.4 we categorize some specific measures according to their primary intended purposes.

There are a variety of formative assessment measures that are drawn from multiple data sources, including students and family members. These common assessments have been selected by teachers through consensus building. Teachers are well aware that they must view assessment from varied and multiple perspectives to gain a thorough understanding of what their students can do.

The sample framework in Table 3.4 illustrates the activities involved in the second phase of the planning process. Worksheet 9 provides a skeletal framework and asks educators to identify appropriate assessments for their assessment plan. Evidence for socialization in L2 or cross-cultural competence (depending on the type of language education program), second language development, and academic learning is drawn from formative and summative measures. Professional development for teachers, along with standard forms for data collection, standard procedures for gathering data, and standard sets of criteria for interpretation of student performance, enhance the usefulness of the data programmatically across classrooms, grade levels, and schools.

Of fundamental importance to the BASIC model is the identification of common or standard assessments, both formative and summative, that can provide adequate evidence for establishing accountability and at the same time give rich portraits of students' learning. The data collected from these assessments not only help individual teachers improve everyday instruction but also, because of their standard practice in the program, provide information about student learning and achievement across classrooms in the program and across programs within a district. Accumulated over time, these data are also used to gauge program effectiveness and program improvement. Table 3.5 identifies specific common assessments used in language education programs in SD 54. These formative and summative assessments constitute the majority of evidence gathered on student development.

Evidence of student progress toward goal attainment is collected, managed, and stored in student portfolios. These pivotal portfolios of student work, maintained over the duration of the language education program, show longitudinal growth of students in language proficiency and academic achievement. Chapter 4 describes specific assessment measures contained in the portfolios, while Chapters 5 and 6 present examples of how teachers in the dual language program and in the transitional bilingual education program in SD 54 use evidence to drive their decision making about classroom and program levels of implementation.

Phase 3: Implementing a Plan

The implementation phase is the most involved, requiring educators to operationalize the frameworks established in the form of concrete plans that can be realized.

Table 3.5 Purposes and Types of Assessments Used in SD 54

	Overall Purpose of Assessment	Type of Assessment*		
		Idiosyncratic	Standard	Standardized
State	Formative			
	Summative		• ISEL[†] • Math portion of ISAT/IMAGE	• ISAT/IMAGE • ACCESS for ELLs®
District	Formative		• Writing samples • IRI • Reading rubric	• MAP
	Summative		• End-of-unit tests	• TerraNova • Other achievement tests (e.g., to identify gifted)
Program	Formative		• Rubrics • Checklists • SOPR • IRI	• MAP
	Summative		• End-of-unit tests • Locally developed performance-based assessments	• IPT • SUPERA
Classroom	Formative	• Teacher observation notes • Teacher-made assessments • Dialogue journals	• Commonly made rubrics, checklists	
	Summative	• Teacher-made tests and quizzes • Performance-based assessments	• Teacher-made tests and quizzes using common assessment criteria • Performance-based assessments using common criteria	

*Assessment is generally not applicable to shaded cells.

[†]Specific measures used by SD54 are described in Chapter 4.

First, a timeline for assessment must be established that includes all selected assessment activities. This schedule of assessment activities, presented month by month, allows teachers to embed performance assessment into instruction, practice using standard rubrics on student samples, and prepare students with test-taking strategies for district and state measures. It guides assessment activities and provides a data management tool for teachers and administrators working in language education programs.

In the third phase, assessment activities selected in the second phase are transferred to a school calendar year. The assessment timeline provides a uniform guide to when and how often each assessment is administered. It also identifies critical common or standard assessments that must be given, in comparison to classroom or idiosyncratic assessments, which are left to the judgment of the teachers. This uniformity is necessary from an assessment standpoint to maintain consistency and determine student progress at regular, preset intervals. Table 3.6 provides the timeline that teachers of ELLs use in SD 54. Worksheet 10 provides a skeletal timeline that educators are asked to complete for their language education program.

Careful planning of assessment allows for ease of implementation. This schedule has to be created with teachers and students in mind, although it also must be sensitive to district or state issues and policies. The schedule is not another piece of paper for a teacher's mailbox. Carefully crafted, the assessment schedule must be coupled with professional development through meetings, coaching, and data-sharing sessions. Teachers have to be aware of what is expected of them and their students, why data-driven decisions need to be the norm, and how data from ongoing assessment are useful in their professional lives. Results need to be articulated, such as in job-alike teams, to gain a thorough understanding of their implications for curriculum and instruction.

When teachers have input into the selection of measures and scheduling of data collection, they become vested in the process. When there are opportunities to exchange information about students and make decisions based on evidence, then teachers become empowered. Ultimately, by becoming increasingly literate in assessment, teachers build their own capacity for improving student learning.

At the beginning of each school year, it is essential to gather baseline data on each student. This initial round of assessment is quite comprehensive and diagnostic so that teachers can place students appropriately and plan for differentiated instruction. Throughout the year, idiosyn-

Table 3.6   The Assessment Timeline for Teachers of English Language Learners in SD 54

	Formative Measures Assessment for Learning	*Summative Measures* Assessment of Learning
August/ September	• Administer the annual informal reading inventory (IRI). • Develop a bilingual individual instructional plan for each student.	• Administer home language survey to all new students. • Administer *WIDA-ACCESS Placement Test* (W-APT, a screener) to determine eligibility for services.
October	• Collect initial writing sample in L2 (and L1) and rate according to district writing matrix. • Administer Fall MAP test.	
November	• Observe students and determine oral language proficiency according to Student Oral Proficiency Rating (SOPR). • Review bilingual individual instructional plan. • Issue report cards.	
December		
January	• Administer *the IDEA Proficiency Test* (IPT). • Administer district math placement test for sixth graders.	
February		• Administer *Assessing Comprehension and Communication in English State to State for English Language Learners* (*ACCESS for ELLs®*), the language proficiency test.
March	• Review bilingual individual instruction plan. • Issue report cards.	• Administer *Illinois Measure of Annual Growth in English (IMAGE),* the academic achievement test for ELLs.
April	• Readminister an IRI for selected students. • Evaluate student's annual progress and determine placement for next academic year using the district Transitional Bilingual Assessment Reference.	
May	• Collect 2nd writing sample in L2 (and L1) and rate according to district writing matrix. • Administer Spring MAP test.	• Administer district standardized achievement test, SUPERA (in Spanish).
June	• Issue report cards. • Administer the *ELL Assessment Kit,* pretest English language proficiency, for summer school.	

cratic and standard types of formative assessments are interspersed. As required, a block of time is devoted to standardized state assessment, both for language proficiency (for ELLs) and for academic achievement.

The most critical undertaking during the implementation phase is the professional development activities so that teachers (1) understand the purpose and administration of an assessment, (2) practice using it in their classrooms, (3) apply the data and information gathered from the assessment to change their own teaching, (4) provide feedback of assessment results to their students, and (5) adapt assessment practices to meet the needs of their students. In a collaborative setting, teachers often peer coach one another and provide valuable suggestions to add to the institutionalization of assessment practices. Through teachers' collaborative work and conversations, assessment practices are continuously improved and made standard.

One advantageous activity during the implementation phase of common formative assessments is for teachers to create anchor samples of student work that typify each level of language proficiency (in L2 and L1) and "proficient" academic achievement at a given grade level. It is important that this collection be stored in a central location in schools so that all teachers can access it and use it. The reasons for maintaining this body of student work include the following:

- To share a unified, single vision of the expectations of students

- To have a pool of student samples for training on establishing inter-rater agreement between teachers on scoring guides or rubrics, thus increasing the reliability and confidence in the results

- To have a comparative reference and resource

- To use at student and teacher conferences, so that parents have an understanding of the relation between their child's performance and that of their peers

- To justify decision making.

Phase 4: Reviewing and Revising a Plan

The assessment frameworks are dynamic in that they evolve over time to meet the changing needs of teachers and students as well as respond to state or district policies that administrators face. Throughout the school year, teachers have opportunities to provide input and feedback up to the end of the cycle, when the framework is revised and updated for the upcoming year. Local data collection efforts that are too cumbersome are discarded in favor of more efficient ones. The use of data to improve teaching, learning, and services to students is closely examined to ensure that decisions are predicated on multiple measures and varied sources of information.

The construction of assessment frameworks and plans is a multiyear endeavor. It requires leadership from administration, experimentation by teachers, and a mutual respect for the process. It is a tremendously complex undertaking to plan, implement, and evaluate assessment practices in language education programs. Collaboration among educators and coordination of effort are key to the success of this intricate and detailed task.

Benefits of a Comprehensive Assessment Framework to Major Constituents

A comprehensive assessment framework for language education programs depicts both a process and product that serve a range of purposes for the different constituents. For administrators, such as assistant superintendents and principals, it is important to have an overall framework that is in concert with those of the school district and state. In this way, language education is integrated into the general educational program. The BASIC model that serves language education programs can readily be expanded and applied to the entire educational arena.

For program administrators, such as directors or coordinators of language education services, an assessment framework that aligns standards and goals with assessment measures establishes underlying program validity. Administrators now have tools to lead their charge, build common formative assessments, plan sustained professional development, and collect valid data on the effectiveness of their programs. Furthermore, they will establish a common language for communicating results and discussing data-driven decisions.

Finally, for teachers, assessment frameworks are reminders of the importance of the use of data generated by their students throughout the school year. While the overall framework offers a general plan in concert with curriculum, the detailed month-by-month picture of standards-based assessment helps frame their instructional practices. Because teachers are integral to the implementation of the BASIC model, their assessment *for* learning contributes to a balanced system that relies on multiple measures for distinct purposes.

The assessment framework presented in this chapter is grounded in a sound set of principles that provide guidance for overall program operation. Information about students' language proficiency and academic achievement is drawn on a formative basis from classrooms and on a summative basis from district- and state-level testing. These qualitative and quantitative data, both in L1 and L2, are both student-centered and teacher-directed to yield a comprehensive profile of student performance.

Questions for Reflection and Action

1. Think about the relationship between standards, assessment, curriculum, and instruction. How do these components of the BASIC model offer you a means to gather information for decision-making?

2. Reflect upon the current assessment practices in your setting. How might you organize formative and summative data into a cohesive assessment framework?

3. Identify key constituents who might contribute to designing and implementing an assessment plan for your language education program. What strategies can you think of to promote collaboration among these constituents?

Using the Pivotal Portfolio to Profile Student Learning

Chapter Overview

This chapter focuses on the components and characteristics of the pivotal portfolio. We review typical assessments included in the pivotal portfolio and explain how these assessments are used to measure students' language and academic growth. Then we describe multiple ways that educators can use the pivotal portfolio as an instructional, evaluation, and reporting tool.

Guiding Questions

- What are the characteristics and uses of a pivotal portfolio in a language education program?
- What kinds of assessments should be included in a pivotal portfolio? What are the criteria that can be used to select assessments for inclusion in the portfolio?
- How can a teacher use the information in the pivotal portfolio to improve student learning?

Key Concepts

- A pivotal portfolio is an organized, systematic collection of critical evidence of students' learning and achievement over time based on common assessments.
- Common assessments selected must be related to the essential learning outcomes in three categories: Language proficiency, academic content learning and cross-cultural competence.
- Clarifying the purpose and use of the pivotal portfolio helps educators construct its components and contents.

Portfolio assessment provides a valid way to gather information on student learning and achievement from multiple sources over time (Gottlieb, 2006; O'Malley and Valdez Pierce, 1996). In this chapter we describe the common assessments of a pivotal portfolio and show how information from the pivotal portfolio can be used to inform decision making in language education programs.

What Is a Pivotal Portfolio?

A pivotal portfolio is an organized, systematic collection of student work that provides authentic evidence of student learning and achievement over a period of time. A critical feature of the pivotal portfolio is that this evidence of student learning and achievement is based on educators' use of common or standard assessments throughout the language education program. When administrators and teachers use common assessments of their students' learning and achievement over time, and when they provide evidence of that learning in a user-friendly portfolio, they create a shared understanding of the strengths and needs of their students. This shared understanding of student strengths and needs then provides a principled basis for focused program and professional development.

In the early 1990s, the use of portfolios was popularized by educators concerned with authentic assessment (i.e., assessment of the individual student's development, not assessment based on norm-referenced testing). Portfolios were used in many content subjects by teachers who embraced performance-based instructional assessment. As explained by Tierney, Carter, and Desai (1991), "some of the values that underlie the use of portfolios include the belief in developing procedures for planning classroom learning that represents what students are actually doing" (p. 41). Teachers can use portfolio information to plan instruction for individual students as well as for groups of students. In addition, the portfolio serves as a historical record of student achievement over time and so can be used for program evaluation.

Individual teachers often make independent classroom decisions about the content of the student portfolio and how it is used. Some teachers use a working portfolio where all student work in progress is kept; others use a showcase portfolio where students choose their best work to feature. The showcase portfolio demonstrates the student's best work and achievement, the working portfolio provides a rich portrait of the student at different stages of learning, with individual strengths and weaknesses. Because portfolios are usually constructed by classroom teachers, the content of portfolios is often limited to the teacher's instructional focus and classroom assessment.

The pivotal portfolio is a hybrid of both the working portfolio and the showcase portfolio, with three main distinctions: in the pivotal portfolio, each teacher gathers what the teachers collectively consider evidence of essential student learning and achievement; all of the teachers use common assessments of that essential student work; and the pivotal portfolio follows the student for the length of the student's career in the language education program. Many teachers choose to maintain both a working portfolio and a pivotal portfolio for each student. Table 4.1 compares the features of working, pivotal, and showcase portfolios.

A pivotal portfolio provides feedback for students as they reflect on their own learning, both as it emerges in the completion of a current task and in relation to the student's history of growth and achievement over time. For teachers, the portfolio provides evidence of each student's learning, growth, and achievement in core subject areas that comes from multiple common assessment sources. Teachers are confident in their assessments of student work because they have collaborated with their colleagues to select common assessments, identified what counts as evidence of essential learning, and learned how to use those assessments consistently for all their students. This assessment information helps teachers differentiate instruction, make adjustments, monitor student progress, and report to parents.

At the program level, patterns of student achievement by subgroups can be collected over time. This information guides program decisions and staff development. Schools can also present a more balanced and defensible report of student progress and achievement to parents and the community by combining summative and formative data that they have collected in students' portfolios over time.

To have optimal utility for students, teachers and administrators, a viable pivotal portfolio must have the following characteristics:

- It must be representative of students' original, authentic work.

- It must include evidence of both growth and achievement, as represented by common formative and summative assessments.

- It must provide a rich portrait of the student's learning over time.

- It must be aligned with the goals and standards of the language education program by having consistent evaluation criteria that allow student work to be compared with learning goals.

- It must have internal reliability with consistent data that can be compared from year to year and from student to student.

- It must have internal validity that addresses the program's mission, goals, and student learning targets.

- It must include ample assessments that can be used by both teachers and students to make classroom decisions related to teaching and learning (Guskey, 2003).

- It must be flexible and comprehensible enough to be useful in answering accountability questions about the program, both internally and externally.

Due to the contextualized nature of the pivotal portfolio, educators need to decide what components are essential for their students' portfolio, with reference to the local school context and the goals of the local educational program. A portfolio for English language learners (ELLs) in a transitional bilingual program, for example, is different from a portfolio for students in a dual language program. Although materials demonstrating English language growth and achievement are included in both, a dual language portfolio includes evidence of more sustained learning in the target language other than English. A dual language portfolio in a Spanish-English program is quite different from a Japanese-English dual language portfolio simply because students develop Spanish literacy at a different rate and sequence than Japanese literacy.

In a dual language program, students have a pivotal portfolio that includes common assessments that are aligned with the program's goals. Unlike other language education portfolios, the one for a dual language program is used to collect data on students' growth and achievement in two languages. In Schaumburg School District 54, this portfolio follows each student from year to year and becomes the student's graduation present at the end of eighth grade. The pivotal portfolio is not only an assessment tool, it is also a historical, cumulative record of the student's career in the dual language program.

Table 4.1 Comparison of the Pivotal Portfolio with Other Types of Portfolios

	Working Portfolio	*Pivotal Portfolio*	*Showcase Portfolio*
Intended purpose	Provides evidence of student work in progress in order to plan instruction	Provides evidence of essential student learning and achievement through time	Provides evidence of student-selected best work to illustrate achievement
Data sources and content	Idiosyncratic classroom-based assessment and current student work samples	Common formative and summative classroom-based assessments used by all teachers Selected student work samples of what teachers consider essential evidence of learning and achievement Required state and federal test results	Selected student completed best work samples at the final phase of learning projects
Value	Provides clues to student's strengths and weaknesses in specific academic subjects during a learning period	Provides a rich portrait of a student as a learner over time in multiple targeted academic subjects and other areas of learning Assessment data are comparable for students across classes in program and across programs in district	Provides authentic evidence of a student's achievement in specific academic subjects after a period of instruction

Through the collaborative process of selecting reliable and valid common assessments, educators construct a pivotal portfolio that serves as the main vehicle for data collection on student learning over time, linking classroom assessment directly to program evaluation. These assessments include summative tests required by state or federal mandates, but, most important, they also include common, formative assessments that are classroom-based and selected or designed collaboratively by groups of teachers for their own instructional purposes, to provide student feedback and guide student learning. Additional contextualized information is also included as supportive evidence to document and enrich each individual student's history and journey as a learner.

Common classroom assessments in the pivotal portfolio are selected based on specific criteria to ensure reliability and validity. They:

- Follow best assessment practices.

- Give useful feedback to students to reflect on their own learning.

- Help teachers make effective, timely instructional decisions.

- Are readily integrated into daily instructional routines.

- Yield information about both student learning growth and achievement.

- Include authentic student work that is performance-based.

Worksheet 11 in the Appendix is a checklist to help educators select and evaluate common assessments to be used in pivotal portfolios.

By collaborating in the selection and design of common classroom assessments, teachers help each other construct a more reliable pivotal portfolio for assessment. In addition, they are also able to use the information in student portfolios to measure and compare student progress from year to year, from group to group, and from context to context. The pivotal portfolio thus becomes the common assessment tool used by all teachers in a language education program to make important instructional decisions and articulate results across grade levels.

Critical Questions about Student Learning and Achievement

The global assessment framework using the BASIC model (see Table 3.3) emphasizes that cross-cultural competence, language proficiency, and academic content standards, aligned with the goals of the particular language education program, are the guideposts framing any effective language education assessment plan. These guideposts also lead to the critical questions that drive the collection, analysis, and interpretation of data on student learning. In language education programs, common assessments in the pivotal portfolio, guided by the BASIC model, provide answers to the following critical questions about student learning:

- How does student language acquisition progress throughout the year and from year to year in listening, speaking, reading, and writing in both first and second languages?

- What is the student's L1 and L2 proficiency level from year to year, individually and compared with that of respective peers?

- How is the student performing in core academic content subjects, such as language arts, math, science, and social studies, throughout the year and from year to year? What are the student's strengths and weaknesses in each academic area?

- How is the student's development of cultural empathy and competence evident in student work through the year and from year to year?

Over time, the collection of evidence in student portfolios can also help answer critical evaluation questions, like the following, that lead to program improvement:

- Are all students in the program as a group attaining first- and second-language proficiency at the expected rate?

- Are the students as a group adequately performing in various academic subjects and meeting state and local standards?

- Do the students as a group demonstrate desired levels of cultural competence as a result of participating in language education programs?

- Are there are any areas of curriculum and instruction that need to be improved to maximize student learning?

Educators in School District 54 use a planning chart to help them build a pivotal portfolio that answers these critical questions. Figure 4.1 is the chart the School District 54 dual language educators used to review and revise the content of the pivotal portfolio for the Spanish-English dual language program.

In an era of increased high-stakes testing, assessment mandated by the No Child Left Behind (NCLB) Act has become state required. School districts and schools are often tempted to use only these data as sole indicators for accountability. The result is a vicious and self-defeating cycle whereby schools struggle with how to raise their scores while forgetting to look at evidence of learning that is most helpful for instructional improvement, namely, formative, classroom-based assessment.

Spanish/English Dual Language Program—Summative Assessment

	Language and Literacy Growth		Content Achievement	
	Native English Speakers	Native Spanish Speakers	Native English Speakers	Native Spanish Speakers
L1	• ISAT Reading and Writing • MAP Reading	• Supera Reading (2nd, 4th, and 6th)	• ISAT Math • MAP Math	• Supera Math (2nd and 4th) • Supera S.S. (6th)
L2	• IPT Spanish • Supera Reading (4th and 6th)	• ACCESS • IMAGE/ISAT Reading • MAP Reading	• Supera Math (4th) • Supera S.S. (6th)	• IMAGE/ISAT Math • MAP Math

Spanish/English Dual Language Program—Formative Assessment

	Language and Literacy Growth		Content Learning	
	Native English Speakers	Native Spanish Speakers	Native English Speakers	Native Spanish Speakers
L1	• ISEL • QRI • Writing Samples w/ Rubric • MAP (Reading)	• ISEL • Flint Cooter • Writing Samples w/ Rubric	• Observation • Teacher Created Quizzes and Tests • MAP (Math)	• Observation • Teacher Created Quizzes and Tests
L2	• Flint Cooter • Writing Samples w/ Rubric • SSL Checklist	• MAP (Reading) • ISEL • QRI • Writing Samples w/ Rubric	• Observation • Teacher Created Quizzes and Tests	• Observation • Teacher Created Quizzes and Tests • MAP (Math)

Figure 4.1 Common assessments for School District 54's dual language program. (Schaumburg Community Consolidated School District 54, Schaumburg, Illinois; reprinted with permission)

In Chapter 2 we discussed the need to balance high-stakes, summative testing with formative classroom measures in an authentic assessment system. The dual language assessment planning chart in Figure 4.1 shows how School District 54 tries to keep that balance in its selection of common assessments used in one of its dual language program. Worksheet 12 is a planning sheet that dual language educators can use to ensure they balance formative and summative assessments of student growth and achievement relative to all program goals in their contexts.

In their book, *Assessment for Learning*, Chappuis, Stiggins, Arter, and Chappuis (2003) make a case for using multiple assessments to guide teachers in their instruction and actively involve students in reflection of their own learning. They recommend balanced assessment systems that include a variety of summative and formative measures to accommodate differences among students and help build student confidence and teacher efficacy. In the current school reality, testing requirements often lead educators to minimize other assessment practices that could be helpful. A comprehensive assessment framework must include both summative and formative assessments.

The selection of common assessments for the pivotal portfolio requires balancing between, on the one hand having sufficient data to give useful feedback to students and to aid teachers in improving daily instruction, and on the other hand acquiring appropriate data to meet external accountability demands. The common assessment measures for the pivotal portfolio are reviewed every two or three years so that changes can be made to reflect new regulations and policies or a new curricular emphasis, or simply to improve the quality of the assessment measures to meet the needs of changing populations of students.

Typically, it is advantageous to build into the portfolio some flexibility for classroom teachers so that they can choose the informal assessments that are most closely aligned with their instruction. Portfolios can also give students a voice as well, by having them select their best work to feature. Because testing mandates often take time, teachers prefer informal measures that can be woven into their daily instruction, such as periodic rating of samples from a writing workshop according to a common writing rubric. The Student Oral Proficiency Rating (SOPR)[1] is an example of an observation instrument that teachers can use to rate

---

[1] The SOPR was developed by Development Associates in Arlington, VA, and adapted from the SOLOM (Student Oral Language Observation Matrix), which was developed by San Jose Unified School District, San Jose, CA.

their students' overall second-language proficiency based on their language use in the classroom, without the burden of teachers having to test each student.

Since assessment practices need to be developmental to be appropriate for students of different ages, the pivotal portfolio is slightly different for younger students than for older students. For example, story retelling may be a way to solicit second-language oral samples from younger students, while an informal interview provides evidence of the second-language oral proficiency of older students.

Over the last 10 years, School District 54, through teacher collaboration, has developed a sample portfolio prototype for every grade level in both the transitional bilingual education (TBE) program and the dual language program. Table 4.2 is a sample prototype portfolio for the TBE program at the primary level, while Table 4.3 is an example of the contents of a sixth-grade dual language portfolio.

Common Assessments: The Building Blocks of a Viable Pivotal Portfolio

As illustrated in Tables 4.2 and 4.3, the essential components of a pivotal portfolio are the common assessments implemented across the language education program. Some assessments are required for evaluation of student achievement (summative), others are selected to help teachers gauge student growth periodically (formative). Required tests can be imposed by local, state and federal policies. To minimize the time consumed by overreliance on testing, we encourage educators to use the results of one test to meet several assessment and evaluation requirements. Common diagnostic assessments, for example, are useful for determining eligibility for intervention programs as well as to inform daily instruction in the classroom.

The common summative and formative classroom assessments discussed in this section fall into one of three categories: oral language proficiency, literacy development, or academic learning. In addition, cross-cultural learning and competence can be measured through informal surveys and observation of students' behaviors in cross-cultural situations. The following discussion describes in detail the measures associated with each assessment category.

Table 4.2 Components of a Pivotal Portfolio in the Transitional Bilingual Education Program in School District 54

Program-Based Common Assessments	Classroom-Based Assessments
W-APT (State-required ELL screener)— Listening, Speaking, Reading, Writing • Administered at entry into program at base building • Administered and scored in January of each year in bilingual classroom	**Academic Performance in Native Language (L1):** • IPT Spanish, when appropriate • L1 writing samples • Performance assessment of academic achievement in L1, as appropriate
ACCESS for ELLs (State-required ELL annual language proficiency test) • Administered February through March of each year in bilingual classroom	
SOPR (Student Oral Proficiency Rating) • Completed in TBE classroom in November of each year • Data collected as natural learning occurs, requiring no special test • Oral proficiency interview (optional)	• Performance assessment for each ESL unit (into English), as appropriate • Audiotaped language samples • Videotaped language samples
Writing Proficiency Matrix • Two writing samples collected and assessed in September and May of each year in the TBE classroom • Data collected as natural learning occurs, requiring no special test or prompt • Both first and last drafts collected and assessed for second graders	• Journal/learning log • Additional writing samples
Individual Reading Inventory (IRI) • Completed in September and April of each year in the bilingual classroom • Running records as part of routine reading instruction	• End of language arts unit tests • Reading observation matrices • Strategic reading assessment, when appropriate • Self-assessment and book log from the ESL program materials • Story retelling
ISEL (State early literacy test) • Administered initially in October and additionally as needed • Report card • Other standardized tests, such as Measure of Academic Progress (MAP), as appropriate	**ISEL** Spanish • Administered as appropriate to gauge L1 reading readiness • Anecdotal/observation notes • Sample of work in various content subjects • Project-based assessment data

Source: Schaumburg Community Consolidated School District 54; reprinted with permission.

Table 4.3 Components of a Sixth-Grade Dual Language Portfolio

Program-Based Common Assessments	Classroom-Based Assessments
W-APT (English) for ELL native Spanish Speakers • Administered at entry into the program	• Performance assessment of academic achievement in Spanish and English for most subjects
IPT Spanish (Spanish language proficiency test) for native English speakers • Administered and scored in January	
ACCESS for ELLs® (state required ELL proficiency test) • administered February–March to ELLs	
SOPR (Student Oral Proficiency Rating in L2) • Completed in November • Data collected as natural learning occurs, requiring no special test	• Performance assessment for each ESL/SSL unit, as appropriate • Digital/video showcase sample of student's L2 proficiency
Writing Proficiency Matrix • Completed in October and May. • Data collected as natural learning occurs, requiring no special test or prompt • Both first and last drafts collected and assessed • Samples must include L1 and L2 for each student and represent various types of writing	• Journal/learning log. • Additional writing samples • Self-assessment when appropriate • Interactive writing journal assessment
Spanish or Japanese Language Checklist • Completed each trimester for all students to indicate student's language competency vis-à-vis each grade-level program goals for the target language	• Teachers' notes on student's progress • Illustrative student work samples
IRI (Individual Reading Inventories) • Completed in Fall and again in Spring if appropriate • Students in Spanish-English program are assessed in L1 and L2 using QRI and Flint Cooter	• End of language arts unit tests • Reading observation matrices • Other diagnostic reading assessment, as appropriate • Self-assessment and book log • Story retelling and running records

Table 4.3 *continues*

Program-Based Common Assessments	Classroom-Based Assessments
Academic Performance Assessment • Report card • Other standardized tests, such as Measure of Academic Progress (MAP), as appropriate • ISAT or IMAGE (state academic achievement tests), administered in April • SUPERA administered to Spanish-English dual-language program students in April in 2nd, 4th, and 6th grades	• Anecdotal/observation notes • Sample of work in both languages in various content subjects • Performance-based assessments using project-based criteria and rubrics • Traditional quizzes and tests

Source: Schaumburg Community Consolidated School District 54; reprinted with permission.

Oral Language Proficiency

In dual language programs, oral language proficiency data (for listening and speaking) are collected, using both summative and formative measures, for English and the target language for language-majority and language-minority students.

- Nationally norm-referenced tests are available for school districts to use to measure their students' second-language proficiency. Some of these commercial tests include the Language Assessment Scales (LAS) and the IDEA Proficiency Test (IPT). These tests are generally given annually and provide yearly oral proficiency growth evaluations for individual students. The IPT and LAS are available in both English and Spanish and provide a relative comparison between languages for students in dual language programs. The use of the IPT test has been essential in helping School District 54 document student language acquisition from year to year and has contributed to a five-year evaluation study of the dual language program (reported in Chapter 7).

- The NCLB Act requires that ELL students take an annual English proficiency test. Although each state chooses its own test, several states, including Illinois (the state in which School District 54 is located), have elected to form a consortium to develop a common assessment in English proficiency based on its English language proficiency standards. Assessing Comprehension and Communication in English State to State for English Language Learners (ACCESS for ELLs), developed by the World-Class Instructional Design and Assessment (WIDA) Consortium (2006), is an example of the new generation of English language proficiency tests.

- There are no large-scale language proficiency tests for low-incidence languages such as Japanese. Consequently, assessments need to be created locally for use in these language education programs.

- The Student Oral Proficiency Rating (SOPR) is an analytic rubric whereby teachers rate students' overall oral proficiency based on classroom observation. Data should be collected biannually: once at the beginning of the year, to establish a baseline, and again at the end of the year, to gauge oral language growth. Because observation occurs in a natural setting, the SOPR provides authentic information about student's oral proficiency.

The Student Oral Proficiency Assessment (SOPA), developed by the Center for Applied Linguistics (CAL) in 1996, has yielded promising program evaluation data in regard to oral second-language proficiency growth of English-Spanish dual language students (Fortune & Arabbo, 2006). The SOPA proficiency rating is a rubric that ranges from junior novice–low to junior advanced–high and includes four major areas of assessment: oral fluency, grammar used in speaking, vocabulary used in speaking, and listening comprehension. The SOPA is currently available in six languages. In addition to the SOPA, the CAL Oral Proficiency Examination (COPE,) from the Center for Applied Linguistics, (2004) is an interview-based assessment adapted from the ACTFL proficiency guidelines of the American Council on the Teaching of Foreign Languages (1985). The COPE is currently available in seven languages.

- Second-language learning checklists that are designed based on program goals are another valid way to gauge student progress, especially for low-incidence languages. In School District 54, based on parents' input, a checklist has been designed for both Japanese as a Second Language (JSL) and Spanish as a Second Language (SSL) students in the dual language program. These checklists serve as benchmarks for second-language learning from grade to grade and meet program expectations of students' target language proficiency at each grade level.

A recent SSL checklist designed for grades K–6 is included as part of Worksheet 13 in the Appendix. It is representative of the local program goals and is aligned with local instructional practices. Because it is constructed collaboratively by teachers based on their observations of student performance in their own classrooms, the checklist sets reasonable expectations. Most importantly, because the teachers have designed this assessment tool to meet their own needs, they take ownership of its implementation. The checklist is reviewed and updated regularly to make sure it is aligned with changing practices and curricular mandates. Educators are encouraged to use and adapt this checklist as appropriate in their dual language programs.

- Story retelling is a strategy for assessing a student's use of descriptive language in narrative form. Students are evaluated according to the richness of the vocabulary used, the details of the description, and fluency. It is a formative means of evaluating oral production of young students within a familiar school routine. This instructional assessment strategy can be easily integrated within language arts teaching.

Story retelling is often used as a part of an individual reading inventory (IRI) to assess a student's listening comprehension. Having students do a story retelling in their first language after reading in their second language can provide an effective check of reading comprehension, especially in the primary grades.

- Informal oral interviews, although time-consuming, provide the most authentic oral language samples of student proficiency because they occur during real interaction in the target language. An interview of this sort is a performance-based assessment that uses a well-designed oral proficiency rubric for interpretation. Depending on the students' proficiency, an informal interview can last from 5 minutes to more than 30 minutes. ACTFL provides training in how to conduct interviews and how to rate the oral proficiency of adult and young adult learners. The ACTFL Proficiency Scale (Breiner-Sanders, Lowe, Miles, & Swender, 1999) is quite useful for conducting oral interviews with older learners and provides a comprehensive framework for assessing second-language oral proficiency. However, as mentioned earlier, the COPE is a more appropriate interview format to use with young children in English-Spanish dual language programs.

Literacy Development

Reading

A renewed focus on reading assessment in general education has led to the development of many kinds of reading assessments for school districts. Although the selection of common reading assessments is often driven by local practices and philosophies in general education classrooms, in dual language settings, consideration must be given to measurement in two languages. The following is a description of reading assessment practices that meet both district-wide needs and second-language program goals.

- Individual reading inventories are useful formative classroom assessments. Administered to students usually twice a year, the multiple performance-based tasks measure student listening and silent reading comprehension, vocabulary knowledge, and phonemic awareness. The resulting profile is an inventory of each student's strengths and weaknesses in reading.

IRIs are advantageous because they can be integrated into a classroom's instructional routine. A teacher may use information from this assessment to plan mini lessons to teach reading strategies, help students select books for independent reading, and identify students who need intervention. Over several years, student IRI profiles show growth and specific areas for targeted instruction. The IRI is an example of an assessment that is mixed in format in that, although it is qualitative in nature, the scores are quantified so that quantitative analysis can be done for groups of students. Many IRIs in English and in Spanish are commercially available, such as the Qualitative Reading Inventory (Leslie & Caldwell, 2001), the Basic Reading Inventory (Johns, 1997) and the Flynt-Cooter Reading Inventory (Flynt & Cooter, 1998). Experienced bilingual teachers can construct similar IRIs for low-incidence languages for use in their classrooms.

- Reading observation matrices have been developed and are widely available for teachers. Most states have a reading rubric reflective of their reading standards that answers state accountability demands and internal program reading goals.

In dual language programs, reading rubrics should be similar but not identical for each target language. In TBE programs, reading rubrics should mirror English language proficiency standards set for ELLs and state language arts standards. Using rubrics is an effective way for teachers to differentiate assessment for their students. Rubrics can be carefully constructed as scoring guides for performance based tasks (Gottlieb, 2006). They can be collaboratively constructed by students and their teachers as a part of setting expectations for learning and evaluating achievement (Arter, 2006b).

- Sample reading responses or reading logs by students, collected and evaluated periodically, provide information about the level and genre of texts read by students as well as their depth of comprehension and engagement in reading. These artifacts provide additional information about the student as a reader that is not available in tests and quizzes, such as the student's attitudes, motivation, and interests.

- End-of-unit tests and quizzes are a convenient and quick means that teachers can use to evaluate whether or not students have mastered particular skills or concepts taught in reading. Sometimes pre- and posttests help teachers assess student knowledge at the beginning of a unit of instruction. They also help students set goals for mastering specific skills.

Writing

Writing assessment is the third component of a comprehensive language assessment portfolio. Traditionally, writing assessment has ranged from simple quizzes to multiple-choice tests that include fill-in-the-blank items, short-answer questions, or lengthy essays written in response to a prompt. In the past two decades, with the emphasis on a multiphasic, recursive writing process (brainstorming, drafting, revising, editing, and publishing), writing assessment has changed to include more authentic student work.

- Writing rubrics that illustrate student performance in each area of writing development can be used to interpret student work. Writing samples of various genres and phases of the writing process are collected and rated according to the established rubrics. Many states have writing rubrics that accompany writing standards for each grade. Local programs can also create rubrics that meet local learning goals in writing. Better yet, teachers can create their own writing rubrics to meet specific writing objectives they have for students within a particular unit of study. Teachers can follow a step-by-step process to collaboratively develop common rubrics to assess student performances in writing (Arter, 2006b).

It is important to agree on a general writing rubric based on the program goals in a particular language. This common program assessment can be used to collect important data about student development in writing from year to year and from target language to target language. Comparisons between groups of students can be made to gauge the rate of growth and level of achievement of students in the area of writing in both their first and second languages.

Interactive journals and learning logs are not scored; however, these samples provide authentic, performance-based evidence of student writing. Interactive journals are samples of authentic writing by students that are shared with the teacher or classmates. Learning logs are records where students write about their interests or summaries of academic knowledge they have acquired in particular subjects. These instructional tools give insight into a student's capabilities as a writer.

Academic Learning

Although traditional tests and quizzes are often used by teachers to assess students' academic learning, it is also important to include examples of student work in the pivotal portfolio to support a teacher's evaluation of student performance. Although not every piece of student work in each content area can be included (these pieces can be contained in the working portfolio and purged at the end of the year), it is advantageous to showcase a variety of good work by students.

- Student samples of their best work can be used to informally gauge the achievement of a student in a particular subject. More important, student work samples collected over time provide illustrations of the process and content of learning. This historical record is quite useful to teachers at the beginning of the year to give them information on the academic status of their new students.

• Performance-based work samples from learning projects and problem-solving tasks are useful and authentic ways to provide information about student learning and exploration of complex concepts. They provide the teacher with glimpses of the depth of understanding of the student in a particular subject, as well as their procedural knowledge (O'Malley and Valdez Pierce, 1996). In project-based learning, students can benefit from using technology to showcase their work, such as in creating PowerPoint presentations, producing video clips to illustrate their learning, or using multimedia to illustrate their findings on a topic. Checklists and rubrics that use content-based criteria can be created to hold students accountable for meeting specific learning objectives in each project. These informal tools can be integrated with instruction and designed by the teacher with student input as they set goals for their own learning at the beginning of each unit (Goodrich, 1996).

• Teacher-generated performance-based assessment, when skillfully constructed to align with learning goals and standards, can be the most valid assessment of students because it reflects what has been taught in the classroom. Whereas traditional tests and quizzes provide evidence of student mastery of specific, discrete skills, performance-based assessment provides much more authentic proof of a student's mastery of complex concepts and skills. Tasks that require students to demonstrate their learning through problem solving or to apply their knowledge to a real-life situation show not only the student's declarative knowledge but also his or her deeper procedural knowledge of the subject. Quality performance assessment tasks meet three basic criteria: (1) the requirements of the task are directly related to learning objectives and include a description of criteria to judge student proficiency on the intended learning targets; (2) the task includes enough evidence or samples of work to sufficiently evaluate student performance; and (3) the task requirements are free of bias that may interfere with the accuracy of the information collected (Arter & Chappuis, 2006).

- Self-assessment strategies such as learning logs, "What I know, want to know, and learned" (KWL) journals, or goal-setting activities can be used to help students monitor their own learning. Student self-assessment and reflection on their own work provides invaluable information about students as learners and the strategies they use in learning. This evidence helps to paint a rich portrait of students and serves as a validity check against other data gleaned from formal test results. Learning logs are a useful tool to encourage students to engage in self-assessment and monitoring, thus helping them develop internal control of their own learning.

- The report card, a mandated tool for reporting student progress in all subject areas to family members, provides overall information about student proficiency achievement (in L1 and L2) in the classroom. Grading for report cards from common assessments that are standard-based is more reliable than a random assignment of numbers or letter grades based solely on each teacher's preferred assessment practices. Wormelli (2006) presents a convincing case for using formative assessment and student self-assessment in the portfolio to construct a fair and valid grading system in the differentiated classroom.

- State- and district-mandated summative achievement test results provide yet another layer of information of student academic achievement. In norm-referenced tests, we can determine a student's standing in a subject vis-à-vis the performance of her peers. Criterion-based tests assess whether or not a student meets established goals or learning standards. Although the results of these tests, usually available long after administration, have limited utility in improving daily instruction, they nonetheless satisfy external accountability demands at the program level.

Other standardized tests, especially those that are formative in nature, can be helpful for teachers to track students' academic progress throughout the year and make instructional adjustments. Once such test is the Measures of Academic Progress (MAP) developed by the Northwest Evaluation Association (2006). It is administered two to three times a year and tests students' progress in reading and math. Educators considering using these tests with ELLs must take into account the students' level of language proficiency. The advantage of using a norm-referenced, Web-based test like the MAP is that it provides highly reliable results on students' growth in academic achievement compared with that of peers in the norming sample, and teachers can access the results within 48 hours. The disadvantage of this benchmark test is that is replicates state testing rather than focusing on students' authentic learning. The Northwest Evaluation Association also provides teachers with instructional guides based on their students' test results through a program called the Des Cartes Learning Continuum (2003). Unfortunately, no such formative, Web-based, norm-referenced tests exist for K–12 students in languages other than English. Consequently, school districts need to rely on other classroom-based data to track students' academic growth.

Cross-Cultural Competence

Insofar as there is virtually no assessment measure of culture learning that is designed for young children, teachers must use informal means to assess student progress in becoming cross-culturally competent. However, there exist some cultural attitude surveys and profiles that are designed for adults that can be adapted to children. The best way to gauge growth in cultural competence is to observe students communicate and problem solve in cross-cultural encounters. Teachers often make anecdotal records of observations about their students' abilities to problem solve and collaborate with people from different cultural backgrounds. In addition, students' attitudes and beliefs can be examined in class discussions when cultural conflicts are topics of exploration. Change in cultural attitudes and beliefs is also reflected in students' writing and gives teachers authentic evidence of their students' thinking. More often than not, students in language education programs have more opportunities than other students to explore cultural learning and to be exposed to cross-cultural training opportunities.

Overall, there is a need to explore how to assess students' culture learning as part of any language education program. In School District 54, teachers use informal surveys to ask students to self-report on their cross-cultural attitudes in comparison to their peers. Although not scientifically based, these surveys are helpful in gauging students' cross-cultural competence and their comfort level when dealing with culturally unfamiliar situations. Dual language programs can also survey students' choice of friends and the development of cross-cultural friendship patterns. For example, at the end of the first three years of the implementation of School District 54's dual language program, a survey was conducted of approximately 50 students. The results indicated that dual language students were more open to forming and maintaining friendships across linguistic and cultural boundaries. These findings have added to the perceived value of the dual language program by teachers and parents. This pattern of openness to cross-cultural friendship has also been observed and noted by teachers and parents. Although this informal measure of student preference on friendship choice is not part of the academic portfolio, it does contribute to the overall value of the language education program.

The common assessments discussed throughout this chapter are a few that School District 54 has used to construct the pivotal portfolio used by all language education teachers. Although not an exhaustive list, these assessment tools have had proven success. First, they have been selected for their utility: information generated from the tools results in improved instruction for students. Second, they represent, to the extent possible, reasonable, defensible assessment practices in various learning contexts. Third, and most important, all measures are aligned with the educational practices of the local school district and the goals of the language education program.

As the emphasis of language education programs changes, as the student population diversifies, or as new external mandates are imposed, the content of the pivotal portfolio needs to be reviewed and revised to best describe the growth and achievement of student learning. The principles of assessment of the BASIC model, discussed in Chapter 2, provide consistency and cohesion for local school districts as revision and changes to the content of the pivotal portfolio occur from time to time. Thus, the pivotal portfolio remains at the core of the BASIC model, an authentic assessment model based on the belief that by systematically selecting, organizing, and using multiple sources of information, educators can better turn data into defensible evidence of student learning.

Using the Pivotal Portfolio to Guide Decision Making: Exiting ELLs

April and May are busy months for the bilingual department of School District 54. At this time, the bilingual teachers sign up for transitioning meetings with a designated administrator in the department to discuss and finalize the last step before exiting select ELLs from the TBE program. The meeting takes approximately 10 to 15 minutes per student. Before the meeting, each teacher updates all evidence of learning in the student portfolio, gathers recommendations from collaborating teachers, and amasses evidence to show that the student has met all program criteria for transition and reclassification.

The crucial question in determining student readiness to transition from the TBE program is, to what extent does the evidence of learning and achievement in language acquisition and academic content show that the student is able to function independently and succeed in a mono-lingual English classroom without specialized language assistance? ELL students may exit from the program only when the evidence in their portfolio indicates they are ready. Program exit criteria required by state rules and regulations are embedded in the pivotal portfolio, and these criteria guide teachers and administrators in their discussion. Table 4.4 outlines the types of evidence educators examine in order to ascertain whether or not a student meets the exit criteria.

Portfolio assessment can be quite cumbersome to manage and implement. In language education programs for ELLs, the result of any system of assessment should have the goal of helping teachers monitor students' growth in English proficiency, make appropriate decisions about the students' academic learning, and set appropriate goals to help students meet criteria to exit the program. The Transitional Bilingual Assessment Reference, or T-BAR, presented in Figure 4.2 is an example of a locally developed tool used in School District 54 to guide instructional decisions for ELL students, from monitoring ESL and academic growth to making the final decision of exiting a student from language support services. The T-BAR is an assessment reference chart that guides teachers in determining the level of English language proficiency of students relative to the program's benchmarks, based on common formative and summative measures. Students are assigned levels of English proficiency—

Table 4.4 Portfolio Evidence Used to Determine Readiness to Exit from a Transitional Bilingual Education Program

General Criteria for TBE Exit	Evidence Based on Common Assessments	Evidence Based on Idiosyncratic Teacher Evaluation
1. Student is orally sufficiently proficient in English to communicate competently in the monolingual English classroom.	Student's Oral Proficiency Rating on the SOPR scale Student's oral proficiency performance on annual state English language proficiency test	Teacher observation notes and anecdotal records
2. Student is reading in English at a level commensurate with typically developing native English-speaking peers of the same grade.	Student's individual reading inventory profile Student's reading ability rated according to district-developed rubric Student's performance in reading on annual state English language proficiency test and state or district reading achievement measures	Classroom-based assessment in reading, such as student's guided reading level or teacher's running records
3. Student is writing in English at a level commensurate with typically developing native English-speaking peers of the same grade.	Student's selected writing samples rated according to district-developed rubric Student's performance in writing on annual state English language proficiency test and state or district writing achievement measures	Teacher's anecdotal notes and classroom evaluation of student's writing throughout the year
4. Student is performing in core academic subjects at a level commensurate with typically developing native English-speaking peers of the same grade.	Student's report card Student's performance in core subjects on state or district formative and summative measures	Teacher's classroom evaluation of student's performance in core academic subjects
5. Student has successfully completed a trial transition period of at least one grading period in a monolingual classroom setting without any TBE support.	Collaborating general education teacher's recommendations for exit with supportive student work samples	Anecdotal records and notes made by teachers about student's progress during the trial transition period

level 1 (beginning), level 2 (intermediate), or level 3 (high)—based on common assessments selected for the portfolio. At least three common assessments from the portfolio are mandatory and representative of each critical area of learning: oral language proficiency, literacy development, and academic learning. Formative, standard assessments conducted at the program level as well as summative standardized tests implemented at the district and state levels are used to determine language proficiency and academic achievement. Worksheet 14 provides a skeletal T-BAR and asks educators to identify criteria that they could use to inform their instructional decisions for the ELLs in their language education program.

In the end, the assessments illustrate the degree to which students can function independently in the English-only learning environment, and thus their readiness for transition or exit from the TBE program. Teachers can easily use results from ELLs' assessments to determine the students' proficiency in English, based on multiple data sources. Teachers also use classroom observation to determine the extent to which students are able to function independently in an English-only academic environment.

In School District 54, once students reach level 3 proficiency they enter a trial transition period that lasts for at least six weeks. During this time, the students receive no language assistance. Collaborative classroom teachers observe the students to ascertain whether they can succeed in the English-only environment without any language support.

As new assessments are adopted and others are eliminated, the T-BAR is amended to reflect current practices in assessment in local language education programs. The T-BAR reflects the assessments that stakeholders in the language education program consider most important. These assessments are required to be used to monitor the progress and achievement of second-language learners.

At the end of this trial transition period, a conference is held between the bilingual teacher and a program administrator, with the optional attendance of collaborating teachers and principals. Most students discussed in transition/exit conferences need to have successfully demonstrated their independence and be ready to take the next step of exiting the program. Discussions with the program administrator help teachers decide whether or not some students need extra time to develop skills in a particular area. The administrator is the facilitator in this process who asks for evidence of "readiness for transition" and helps teachers come to a reflective decision about a student's need for

L2 Oral Proficiency	L2 Reading and Writing Proficiency	L2 Academic Functioning Level
Level I **IPT** NES or LES ------------------------------------ **ACCESS** for ELLs® Level 1 or 2 ------------------------------------ **SOPR** Level 1 or 2	**IPT** NER/NEW (Pre-Reader/Writer) ------------------------------------ **IMAGE** Beginning ------------------------------------ **ACCESS** for ELLs® Level 1 or 2 ------------------------------------ **IRI:** Independent—3 or more levels below grade ------------------------------------ **SD 54 Writing Proficiency Matrix** Level 1 or 2	Unable to function independently in a monolingual English setting in most or all academic subjects.
Level II **IPT** LES ------------------------------------ **ACCESS** for ELLs® Level 2 or 3 ------------------------------------ **SOPR** Level 2 or 3	**IPT** LER/LEW (Beginning Reader/Writer) ------------------------------------ **IMAGE** Strengthening ------------------------------------ **ACCESS** for ELLs® Level 2 or 3 ------------------------------------ **IRI:** Independent—2 or 3 levels below grade ------------------------------------ **SD 54 Writing Proficiency Matrix** Level 3 or 4	Able to function in a monolingual English setting with some tutorial help in social studies, math, and science. ------------------------------------ Report card indicates near average academic functioning with instructional modifications.
Level III **IPT** FES ------------------------------------ **ACCESS** for ELLs® Level 4 ------------------------------------ **SOPR** Level 4	**IPT** CER/CEW (Beginning or Early Reader/Writer) ------------------------------------ **IMAGE** Expanding ------------------------------------ **ACCESS** for ELLs® Level 4 ------------------------------------ **IRI:** Independent—1 level below grade ------------------------------------ **SD 54 Writing Proficiency Matrix** Level 5 or 6	Able to function independently at grade level in a monolingual English setting in most academic classes. ------------------------------------ Report card indicates near average academic functioning with minimal accommodations.

Figure 4.2 School District 54 transitional bilingual assessment reference (T-BAR). (Schaumburg Community Consolidated School District 54, Schaumburg, Illinois; reprinted with permission)

L2 Oral Proficiency	L2 Reading and Writing Proficiency	L2 Academic Functioning Level
Level III/TR **IPT** FES --- **ACCESS for ELLs®** Level 5 --- **SOPR** Level 5	**IPT** CER/CEW (Early Reader/Writer) --- **IMAGE** Transitioning --- **ACCESS** for ELLs® Level 5 --- **IRI:** Independent—at or approaching grade level --- **SD 54 Writing Proficiency Matrix** Level 6	Able to function independently at grade level in a monolingual English setting in all academic classes. --- Report card indicates average or above average academic functioning --- Scores at 45th percentile or above in standardized academic achievement tests.

Figure 4.2 *continues*

bilingual services, using the T-BAR as a reference. Once the decision is collaboratively reached, parents are informed.

Every year, about 10% of ELLs in the school district exit the TBE program. With portfolio assessment used as the cornerstone for decision making, the results of the common assessments in the portfolio are pivotal in helping teachers make this critical benchmark decision on the student's behalf. The effectiveness of the collaborative process of gradually transitioning ELLs in School District 54 into the English-only classroom has been documented; Wagner (2001) found that collaborative decisions based on portfolio assessment solidify the quality of language services for ELLs.

The pivotal portfolio, packed with multiple types of evidence of student learning, provides ample information for teachers and administrators to help decide whether an individual ELL is ready to exit the local TBE or ESL program and be successful in the monolingual English-speaking classroom environment. It also serves as a tool to discuss individual student progress with students and parents. Using assessment information in the portfolio, teachers can work with parents and students to chart realistic expectations and individual learning plans to help students achieve language proficiency and academic achievement. This evidence-based instructional practice guarantees that each ELL who exits from the language education program is sufficiently proficient in their second language and can succeed academically in the all English environment.

Since documents in the pivotal portfolio can accumulate over the years, there needs to be a systematic, efficient way to summarize and record student growth and achievement from year to year. To address this need, School District 54 uses a cumulative record-keeping device to summarize the history of the student's assessment at a glance. This form, included as part of Worksheet 15 in the Appendix, is reviewed periodically. An electronic version of this form is being explored to make the student's assessment history even more accessible to students and teachers.

The next three chapters explore the power of the pivotal portfolio. Chapters 5 and 6 show how teachers use information from the pivotal portfolio to make instructional decisions, and how program administrators use the same data to make program and curricular improvements. Chapter 7 illustrates how educators can use assessment data for program evaluation and improvement.

Questions for Reflection and Action

1. Think about how you collect and use assessment data in your school district. Where is the data stored? To whom are they most accessible? Who uses the results and for what purposes? Are data organized in a way that all constituents (teachers, students, administrators, parents) have easy access to pertinent information necessary for their specific decision-making?

2. If you were to construct a pivotal portfolio for students in your language education program, what would be your criteria? What assessments would you include in the portfolio and why? What interesting features would you add to your pivotal portfolio to make it useful in your context?

3. Imagine that you are a classroom teacher in a school district like School District 54. How would you use information available to you in the pivotal portfolio to plan your classroom instruction and give feedback to students and parents?

Using Evidence to Drive Decision Making in Dual Language Programs

Chapter Overview

In this chapter, a dual language teacher and a dual language program coordinator recount their experiences as they use evidence from the pivotal portfolio to drive decision making on the classroom and program levels. Mrs. Hernandez describes how she uses data collected through common assessments to plan instruction and guide her students' learning as well as to report their progress to parents. Mrs. Meyer shows how assessment data can direct professional development for teachers, inform policy, and strengthen advocacy efforts.

Guiding Questions

- What are the advantages of using information from the pivotal portfolio to set learning goals for students?
- How does collecting and rating writing samples help teachers guide students' writing development in two languages? Compare this assessment strategy with using results from a writing test.
- How can educators use information from students' pivotal portfolios to plan professional development and make improvements in a language education program?

Key Concepts:

- The pivotal portfolio is the assessment tool that anchors instructional and learning decisions at the classroom level.
- Teachers should have professional flexibility in determining how they use assessment information in the portfolio to meet the needs of individual students and help them reach their own learning benchmarks.
- At the program level, assessment information gleaned from students' portfolios provides authentic and rich evidence of students' learning to guide relevant professional development to improve instruction and clarify curricular focus.

This chapter presents the first-hand experiences of two of the professionals who implement the assessment and accountability plan in the dual language program in Schaumburg School District 54. In this chapter we meet Mrs. Rocio Hernandez and Mrs. Danette Meyer and see how they use assessment for learning at the classroom level and the program level. Mrs. Hernandez is one of the fifth- and sixth-grade dual language teachers. She teaches Spanish language arts and science and social studies in Spanish, while a team teacher is responsible for teaching the other content areas to the same students in English. Mrs. Meyer is the facilitator of the dual language program. She coordinates program and staff development. She is the teachers' first program resource and coach as they implement daily instruction. She leads teams of teachers to develop curriculum and district-based assessments that are used in the dual language program. We use Mrs. Hernandez's and Mrs. Meyer's real names with their permission, and we use pseudonyms for the students they discuss.

This chapter shows how these dual language educators collect different types of assessment data, turn the data into useful information or evidence, and take instructional action based on that evidence. The chapter features the strategic uses of information systematically gathered in the pivotal portfolio by teachers and students to improve learning and teaching. It illustrates how educators use multiple common assessments to provide authentic evidence of student learning, guide staff development, and improve the program. The chapter also highlights the collaborative nature of decision making by teachers and administrators in School District 54.

Assessment for Learning in Mrs. Hernandez's Class

Mrs. Hernandez was asked to respond to several questions about how she uses assessment data to inform instruction in her dual language classroom. The following is her account of how she uses evidence of student growth and achievement to promote ELLs' and English speakers' second language acquisition, biliteracy development, and academic learning in two languages. She also explains how she encourages students to take responsibility for their own learning.

A teacher daily undertakes a journey that is filled with rich experiences and knowledge when she engages in teaching. The knowledge that I acquire every day as a teacher comes with my accumulating experience with teaching, with continuous professional development, but most importantly by getting to know each of the students I have in front of me.

One of the most important factors in teaching for me is the importance of getting to know my students. Assessment is a tool that teachers use to constantly learn about their students. I also use assessment to reflect on different instructional strategies that I implement.

Our dual language student pivotal portfolios include several common assessment tools that measure academic growth in all areas in both English and Spanish. These portfolios travel with students from grade to grade and are excellent for building continuity and accountability in student assessment. If anyone has a question about how a student is doing or how a program is working out, all they have to do is refer to the portfolio. Most important, portfolio assessment is a tool that guides our instruction, no matter what instructional approach or program is being implemented. It gives classroom teachers the answers to the following critical questions as we face our students each day: How is student x doing in the classroom? What I am going to teach tomorrow, next week? How do I know that what I am doing is helping all students learn?

My students also use the information in their portfolio to help set their own learning goals and to monitor their own learning. I discuss assessment results with my students on a regular basis in order to guide them in setting realistic goals for themselves. At parent-teacher conference time, the portfolio gives both my students and me ample evidence to plan for our student-led conferences.

I write about four particular students in this chapter: Javier Campos and his language acquisition, Lorena García and her writing abilities, Carrie Southerland and her academic learning, and Rebecca Flint and her reading skills. Through these accounts, I demonstrate how I use assessment information from the pivotal portfolio to differentiate my instruction for each of my students.

Using Language Proficiency Test Data to Promote Second Language Acquisition

Javier Campos is a fifth-grade student in the dual language program. He has been in the program since kindergarten. He is a native Spanish speaker. Both at home and in school, he interacts with family and friends in both English and Spanish. Javier's parents are limited English speakers; therefore, he communicates predominantly in Spanish with them. Javier is a balanced bilingual child communicatively. He is creative and has a sense of humor. This is clearly evident in his writing. Javier is more of an auditory and kinesthetic learner. He is a child who, like most students, is eager to share his personal experiences and knowledge with the rest of the class. He is a young teenager who loves taking risks both socially and academically. During class meetings, he has frequently shared information about his home life experiences, wishes, and goals. Javier has strong interests in music and art. He often participates in our school's talent shows. Since Javier is an ELL, he has taken the IDEA Proficiency Test (IPT) test since kindergarten as an assessment of his language growth in English. Table 5.1 summarizes his IPT performances from kindergarten to fifth grade.

The IPT is a criteria-based second-language proficiency test that yields information about a student's learning growth and performance in a second language in the areas of oral, reading, and writing production. Table 5.1 indicates Javier's language growth in oral language, reading, and writing production in his second language, English. Javier grew from a non-English speaker in kindergarten to a fluent English speaker in third grade. As a teacher reviewing Javier's IPT results, I made the following interpretation. When Javier was in kindergarten, he was able to orally identify high-frequency words in English related to topics such as items in the classroom, food, clothing, and weather. As he grew older and was exposed to more academic and content language in English, the data from the IPT show that he was able to read short stories and to use higher academic and content language. Javier is now capable of using complex sentences with higher-level discourse. Moreover, when analyzing the IPT, it shows that he grew from a limited English writer in second grade to a competent English writer in fourth grade. Therefore, it shows that his oral proficiency leads to both reading and writing proficiency.

September and October are very busy months for teachers in the dual language program. We initially learn about our students' academic and behavioral skills, strengths, and weaknesses. I review the IPT data for the purposes of making instructional decisions for individual and groups of students that can be implemented in my classroom. For example, I compare Javier's IPT performances with those of other students in my class in order to place Javier in appropriate reading and academic groups for

Table 5.1 Javier's Growth in English as a Second Language (K–5) as Measured by the IDEA Proficiency Test (IPT)

	IPT Oral Proficiency Level and Designation	*IPT Reading Score and Designation*	*IPT Writing Score and Designation*
K	C—Non English Speaker		
1	E—Fluent English Speaker		
2	F—Fluent English Speaker	45—Competent English Reader	16—Limited English Writer
3	F—Fluent English Speaker	50—Competent English Reader	18—Competent English Writer
4	Oral test exempted. Student reached highest proficiency at 3rd grade.	42—Competent English Reader	17—Competent English Writer
5	Entire test battery exempted. Student reached highest proficiency at 4th grade.		

learning projects. I need to provide a student like Javier with a lot of oral language, reading, and writing in short, with rich academic and social learning experiences in English.

Even though Javier has reached the highest oral proficiency on the IPT, he still needs to be exposed to a lot of content vocabulary through the integration of reading and writing across the curriculum to continue strengthening his English academic abilities. Academic English proficiency of ELLs, as in the case of Javier, still needs to be nurtured even after they have reached the threshold necessary to participate in an English-dominant environment. I have also exposed Javier to high interest quality literature from all genres in English through teacher read-alouds, shared reading, guided reading at his instructional level, and independent reading and writing experiences. Javier is well on his way to full academic proficiency in his second language, well beyond the language proficiency indicators on his IPT chart. In addition, because we are in a dual language program, I continue to encourage Javier to develop better reading and writing skills in his native Spanish, which is his dominant language.

Using Writing Assessments to Develop Writing in Two Languages

Lorena García is native Spanish-speaking student in fifth grade. Lorena is a hard worker and always willing to help others. She has an excellent attitude toward school. She is involved in many extracurricular activities, such as Girl Scouts, the student council, World Leaders, and the school store. Lorena lives with both mother and father and three siblings. Lorena usually shares with the class how all her siblings are very loving and caring toward each other. Lorena tends to be a tactile and kinesthetic learner. She has strong interests in writing and reading.

The use of formative assessments, such as the writing proficiency matrices and writing conference logs, helps classroom teachers gain information about individual student's learning, and they also provide a richer portrait of the student as a learner.

Lorena Garcia has been a strong writer since the beginning. In first grade, Lorena produced the writing sample shown in Figure 5.1. The writing sample shows that she was a very strong writer even as a first grader. Using the School District 54 Bilingual Writing Rubric, Lorena's first-grade teacher rated the sample as highly competent (Fig. 5.2). This rubric shows that she is focused and organized. Lorena's writing sample has a clear introduction and conclusion, and, most important, she is showing that the writing is for a real purpose, meaningful. Lorena has a real audience. As a reader, you can hear her voice as an author.

A closer examination of her writing sample shows that Lorena made inter-linguistic errors typical of dual language students. For example, it is very interesting to note that Lorena wrote Mra. *to indicate* Mrs. *It is very natural for many native Spanish-speaking students like Lorena to write* Mrs. *as* Mra. *since in Spanish it is* Sra. *Lorena also wrote* the *as* de, *although she changed it later.*

As a fifth-grade teacher, these and other past writing samples and rubrics gave me valuable information about Lorena as she learned to become a bilingual writer. It provided me with actual evidence about her strong writing history. Using this information, I can plan for instruction to help Lorena grow in her writing in both languages.

Lorena in fifth grade is expanding her writing in English and Spanish in various genres—legends, fairy tales, poems, essays, autobiographies, articles, and tall tales. Included here are samples of Lorena's versatile writing, including her autobiography, written in English (Figure 5.3), and

Mra. Valdes
B/05

I think Mra. Valdes
shold win. Becous Mra.
Valdes takes care
of dthe students.
And she is a great
Prensepal. And that ways
I think Mra valdes shod win.

Figure 5.1 Lorena García's first-grade writing sample. See the accompanying writing proficiency matrix in Figure 5.2.

ENGLISH WRITING PROFICIENCY MATRIX*

Student's Name _____ Grade __1__ School __MacArthur__

Writing Type __Persuasive__ Rated by _____ Date __5/02__

DIRECTIONS: For each of the 5 categories below at the left, mark an "X" across the box that best describes the student's abilities.

	EMERGENT(1)	NOVICE(2)	DEVELOPING(3)	COMPETENT(4)	SUPERIOR(5)
FOCUS	No main idea or topic.	Unclear topic, with some main ideas stated. Ideas are unrelated and not explicitly connected.	Fairly clear topic. Main ideas stated but not developed / Elaborated. Irrelevant details. Lacks conclusion / Irrelevant conclusion.	Clear topic. Central idea/purpose is explicitly announced in the opening and maintained. Clear conclusion does not contradict opening. **[X]**	Very clear topic. Includes topic sentence(s) with all main ideas stated. Relevant and integrated details. Clear and relevant conclusion.
SUPPORT	Little to no support of topic. Insufficient writing.	Support attempted but undeveloped. May be inaccurate or inappropriate. Insufficient writing.	Most of major elements are supported with general statements. Elaborations and explanations without integration.	Accurate but incomplete support of topic. Elaborations and explanations are credible, specific and logical. **[X]**	Specific elaborations and explanations included with accurate and credible details integrated to show support of topic in depth.
ORGANIZATION	Lack of organization and logical sequencing.	Unclear organization with some logical, but incomplete sequencing. Limited number of transitional words. Inappropriate paragraphing.	Loose organization with some transitional words/phrases used correctly. Some appropriate paragraphing.	Clear organization with logical sequencing and development. Adequate transitional phrases. Appropriate paragraphing. Minor digressions may exist. **[X]**	Very clear organization with fully developed, logical ideas that are complex and interrelated. No digressions.
STYLE	Meaning obscured by imprecise/limited vocabulary. No apparent sentence structure.	Run-on/fragmented sentences. Non-specific vocabulary that generalizes meaning.	Simple sentences; some run-ons/fragments; little variety in sentence structure. Adequate vocabulary, with appropriate use of technical language. **[X]**	Most sentences clearly written with some variety in sentence structure. Accurate use of technical vocabulary. Appropriate use of writing type/genre.	Clearly written, complete sentences, demonstrating a variety of sentence structures. Creative use of vocabulary. Exhibits skillful use of writing type/genre.

Copyright: Schaumburg Consolidated School District #54 10/95

* This rubric was developed to assess writing proficiency of ESL students.

Figure 5.2 English writing proficiency matrix for Lorena García's writing. (Schaumburg Consolidated School District 54; reprinted with permission)

My Autobiography

What is your life about? My life started in November 13, 1994. I was born in the hospital Metropolitan. The Metropolitan hospital is located in San Antonio, Texas that is the state I was born in. My favorite colors are green and pink. When I started pre-school is when I learned English. I had to move from Skokie, Chicago to Hoffman Estates. My sister skipped kinder, however I went to kinder and that is where I met all my friends I know now. My teacher for kinder was Mrs. Mosquera. My first grade and second was Mrs. Medina. My third grade teacher was Mrs. Rosales. My fourth grade teacher was Ms. Garcia and my fifth grades teachers are Mrs. Hernandez and Ms. Beaty. When I entered fifth grade I moved again to Schaumburg. The clubs that I'm in right now are girl scouts, world leaders, band, after school band, and battle of the books. For band I play the clarinet, I would like to learn how to play the guitar. In my life there has been ups, downs, embarrassing, and funny moments. The best day in my life in the year 2006 was when I heard my niece talk to me for the first time on the phone. The worst day was when I heard my uncle Beto died in Mexico. The most embarrassing moment was when I called my grandpa dad. The funniest day would probably be when I tripped my sister and she fell down and almost cried but started to laugh. My life to me has been kind of interesting. Oh, before I forget my family is Juan, my dad, Marisela, my mom, Liliana, my sister, Me, Carla, my sister, Güero, my dog and my niece Analyah my sister Liliana's baby.

Thank You

Figure 5.3 Lorena García's fifth-grade autobiographical writing in English.

a written retelling, in Spanish, of a legend about San Patricio (Saint Patrick) that she had read in Spanish (Figure 5.4).

My decisions on what to teach in writing depend on what a student is doing well and what she or he can do better. At the beginning of the year, I look at Lorena's writing proficiency matrix and her past writing samples as starting points. This information helps me get an initial idea of Lorena as a writer.

I confer with my students on a regular basis to give them feedback about their writing as they progress. In addition to the writing proficiency matrix, I use a conference log to keep notes of writing conferences with Lorena. These notes add to the portrait of a student as a writer and give me richer information to plan for instruction. I use these notes to guide my conversations with individual writers as I respond to their writing.

¿Que es lo que deberas paso el dia de San Patricio?

¿Que deberás paso el día de San Patricio para que sea el día San de Patricio? Esta leyenda pasó el 1988 en Irlanda Había un día un niño que se llamo Patricio. El era un duende. Su sueño era a ayudar a la gente de su país, Irlanda. —Quiero ser un santo para la gente de mi pueblo.— dijo Patricio. Un día el papá de Patricio murió y el no pudo ser nada para ayudar lo. Desde ese día Patricio fue a la iglesia a confesarse y a ayudar al padre. Un día el padre vio que Patricio estaba llorando. —¿Qué tiene el niño más voluntario del mundo?— preguntó el padre. —Padre a ver si tu me puedes ayudar, ¿qué ago para que sea un santo para la gente de vuestro pueblo?— lo preguntó Patricio al padre. —Eso solo te lo puede contestar la Virgen Maria— le respondió el padre.

    Patricio no entendió lo que dijo el padre. Después de unos días Patricio fue a la iglesia para rezar y ayudar al padre. Pero el padre no estaba allí. Entonces Patricio le pidió a la virgin que le diera una señal para convertirse en un santo. Después, ¡vio que un niño estaba atrapado en un hoyo! Patricio de repente empezó a tratar de quitar todas las piedras de encima. Escucho que el niño gritaba —¡Auxilio!— También gritaba —¡Ayuden por favor!— Patricio estaba desesperado y el le gritaba al niño — ¡Ya llego ayuda!— le gritó Patricio. —¡A horita te saco de allí!— Patricio también gritaba ayuda para un adulto. Antes de que se diera cuenta, ¡Patricio vio el saco al niño del hoyo! Desde ese día el Marzo 17 es y siempre será el día de San Patricio.

¡Feliz Día de San Patricio!

Figure 5.4 Lorena García's fifth-grade written retelling of a legend in Spanish.

When reviewing my conference log notes on all students, I can also find patterns of errors or common needs of my students that I can incorporate into my lessons about writing.

I usually start my daily writing workshop with a whole-class message where I intentionally teach an author's craft or editing lesson, followed by student conferences, then a small guided writing or a shared writing experience. From my experience, students love and are very excited to see their teacher writing about her own topics during shared writing and during the morning message. When I write my own stories, my main focus is to model a revision or an editing lesson that I want the whole class to learn or a skill that I see my whole class needs. For example, I might concentrate on adding more details to a piece, organizing my ideas, staying focused, choosing a topic, or using interesting vocabulary. I might also include in my writing the use of interesting leads, dialogue, author's tone/ mood, onomatopoeia, metaphors, and setting or character development. My lessons depend on what I see my students need and what they are struggling with during our writing workshop. I decide which lessons I am going to teach to the whole class or in small, guided writing groups from the data gathered from the conference logs I keep during student conferences.

While students are doing the writing, I meet with one student for a quick one-on-one writing conference. When students have a conference with the teacher, they bring a piece of writing they are working on or one they would like to publish. I use a small notebook for every child as that student's writing conference log. When students meet with me, I usually affirm their successes before they hear where we need to improve. I try to provide descriptive rather than evaluative feedback to students during their writing process. Figure 5.5 shows a sample conference log I kept on Lorena (written in Spanish). During this writing conference, I learned and shared with Lorena that her strengths include writing with a specific audience in mind, that she establishes a theme in her poetry, that she is very persuasive in her articles, that she includes dialogue and interesting leads. On the other hand, some areas that we need to work on are using synonyms and other literary devices such as alliteration and metaphors. As I

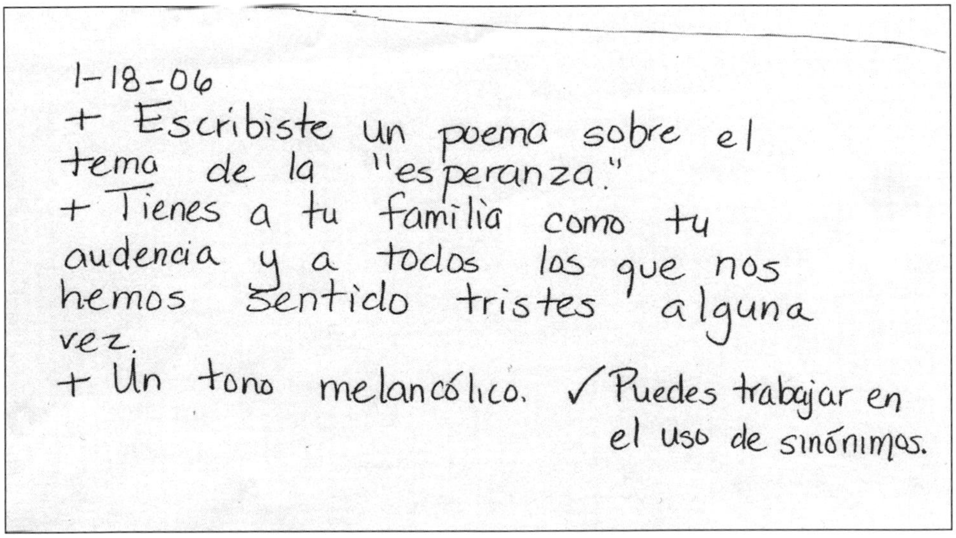

1-18-06
+ Escribiste un poema sobre el tema de la "esperanza."
+ Tienes a tu familia como tu audencia y a todos los que nos hemos sentido tristes alguna vez.
+ Un tono melancólico. ✓ Puedes trabajar en el uso de sinónimos.

Figure 5.5 Conference log for Lorena García, written by Mrs. Hernandez.

am having writing conferences with the students, I plan and decide what, how, and when I am going to teach a particular skill to them. This ongoing, informal assessment guides my daily writing instruction. It gives me rich information about my students as writers, their skills and abilities, and, most important, their interests and dislikes, their concerns, and what motivates them to write more.

I use the information that I learn through my conferences with my students about their writings to suggest ideas or new strategies, or to help them explore a new topic for their writing. Thus, the information is also useful to my students as they learn to become independent, capable writers at their own pace.

Usually students in my classroom choose their own writing topics and are required to do a lot of writing. I have found that being able to choose their own topics helps students become self-motivated, independent writers. I try to present writing to my students not as a forced task but rather as something meaningful and purposeful. To make writing meaningful and purposeful, the integration of literature has also been very beneficial for all my students because they are exposed to authentic literature and how authors really write. Writing conference logs information sometimes aids me in the selection of literature that may be both beneficial and interesting to my students.

I want my students to feel the experience of writing as real authors do. Consequently, I often asked students to share their best writing with the class. Lorena is always willing to share her latest creative work. I believe that Lorena, based on her writing history, is on her way of becoming a powerful writer. For Lorena and for all my other students, I rely heavily on my informal log notes, the students' multiple writing samples, and rubrics to guide my coaching, and on the conferences with my students to help them add to their literary toolbox as they each learn to become an effective bilingual writer. I sometimes make rubrics with my students, using student-friendly terms to better communicate my expectations.

Worksheet 16 in the Appendix asks teachers to use the writing proficiency matrix that School District 54 developed for second language learners to rate Lorena's autobiographical writing in English, and brainstorm her strengths and needs at this point in her writing development. Then teachers are invited to apply this process to assess the writing of their own second language learners, and use their assessment to drive their decisions about instruction.

Using Multiple Criteria to Assess Academic Learning and Set Individual Goals

Carrie Southerland is a fifth-grade native English-speaking student. She has been in the Spanish-English dual language program since she was in kindergarten. She is the first child in her family to be a part of a dual program. Carrie has had the pleasure of traveling to several Spanish-speaking countries. She is extremely proud of being bilingual and uses her bilingual skills in and out of the classroom. Carrie tends to be a visual and kinesthetic learner. She is very involved with technology and is a member of the Production/Technology Club.

As a teacher in the dual language program, I use multiple sources of data to help assess the academic performance of my students in their native language and second language. The information gleaned from multiple assessments is used collaboratively with the students to help evaluate their academic performance and to set individual student learning goals. This individual goal setting is a part of the student-led conference that began to be implemented at MacAthur School in 2004. During parent-teacher conferences, students share their portfolios with their parents, discuss their own progress based on evidence in the portfolio, and set new goals for the upcoming grading period.

Carrie's portfolio that she shared with her parents includes classroom-based assessments and formal test scores, such as results from the end of the unit social studies tests, her language arts projects evaluated using a teacher-made rubric, sample works from her language arts and social studies projects, sample works from her science project, and her most current ISAT scores. The work samples in the portfolio represent all areas of the curriculum and incorporate many targeted skills.

Carrie's portfolio reflects her high academic performance in all areas. Not only does she retain and recall relevant information, but her work samples also show that Carrie applies higher thinking skills as she uses good problem-solving techniques, approaches challenges logically, and applies concepts to new situations. Carrie's most recent Illinois test results shows that in third grade, she exceeded state standards in reading (raw score: 194) and in math (raw score: 191) and she met state standards in writing (raw score: 28). In fourth grade, Carrie also participated in the Supera test to evaluate her academic functioning in her second language, Spanish. She scored in the 60th percentile in reading and in the 50th percentile in math.

By sharing test results as well as the most current student work samples and other classroom-based assessment, Carrie and I are able to give her parents a much richer and more evidence-based report of her progress and achievement than showing them a simple test score or a grade on a report card. I believe that by showcasing their portfolio through goal setting, every child can show his or her parents real evidence of current progress and accomplishments in the first and second languages.

Student-led conferences also help students set individual learning goals and hold them accountable for these goals in front of their parents and teachers. This practice when implemented requires a lot of time to prepare students before they are able to lead the conference with their parents. One of the tools that I use to help my students is the conference notes sheet. Students use a conference notes sheet to guide their conversation with their parents. Figure 5.6 shows Carrie's conference notes sheet, which includes goals that Carrie has established together with her teachers in the areas of reading, writing, and math in English and Spanish. It also describes the action plan that she will take, with specific steps she will follow to improve the skills that she needs to work on to achieve her own learning goal.

Setting one's own learning goal requires a lot of reflection on the students' part and a lot of guidance from their teachers. The students' own learning goals must also align with the general program goals, the curriculum set by the district in order to meet state standards in each content subject. To help students set appropriate goals, I use the skills checklist for each content subject for each grade level. The skills checklist is collaboratively developed by classroom teachers using the program goals, the district curriculum, and state learning standards as guides.

Before students brainstorm a list of goals they want to accomplish throughout the year, they are asked to complete a skills checklist for each academic area. In the skills checklist, students independently complete a chart by checking the box that best describes their current skill in a particular academic area, based on set criteria. After working independently on this task, students meet with their teachers. The teachers and the students work collaboratively to decide what the rating is for each skill, based on set criteria. Figure 5.7 shows a sample is a skill list for reading used with fifth graders that Carrie Southerland filled out in preparation for her student-led conference with her parents.

Once the skills checklist is complete, students use this information to set their own learning goals in each content subject with the guidance of their teachers. When students set academic goals, they learn to accept re-

Conference Notes Sheet

Name: _____ Section: _____

Subject/Work Habit/Social Skill: Sra. Hernandez Reading

Goal (Skill I will work on) My goal is to describe character development plot and resolution be

Action Plan (How I will improve this skill) Re-read the passage slower. Use my reading notebook and reading logs. Write many summaries

Subject/Work Habit/Social Skill: Writing

Goal (Skill I will work on) My goal is to work on ary sentence structure.

Action Plan (How I will improve this skill) I can take a little more time writing and revising and practice at home.

Subject/Work Habit/Social skill: El Srta. Beaty Math

Goal (Skill I will work on) To work on problem solving.

Action Plan (How I will improve this skill) I will do problems step by step, re-check, and practice at home more often.

Conference Notes   Name: _____

Ending Statements

I am proud of . . . My work effort in school because I try very hard.

I will try . To work on taking a little more time in doing things so the outcome is very good.

The most important thing I learned so far this year was . Quick division.

Figure 5.6 Carrie Southerland's conference notes sheet. See the accompanying reading skill list in Figure 5.7.

sponsibility for monitoring their own learning and reporting the parents how they are doing in school, the progress they are making. Moreover, through the practice of self-assessment and student-led conferences, we teach students the basic principles of accepting responsibility for their work in school.

As a teacher, I also use the same checklist and criteria to assess student's academic performance and make instructional decisions. Thus, the skills checklist is an assessment tool that is used for student self reflection, for evaluating student's progress, and ultimately to hold individual students accountable for their own learning.

Carrie's portfolio, with multiple sources of data, has been pivotal in helping us paint for her parents a rich portrait of her academic achievement as a student. Rather than relying only on test scores, we have an array of summative assessment data, coupled with student work samples and classroom-based formative assessments. The portfolio also provides considerable evidence that allows Carrie to show her parents in concrete

Skill List		Name: _____

Complete the chart by checking the box that rates your skill the best.

Reading	I am good at	I am ok at	I can improve on
Read and learn the meanings of unfamiliar words: Root words, prefixes and suffixes.	✓ ✓		
Read a variety of literary forms.	✓ ✓		
Describe character development, plot and resolution.	✓	✓✓	
Read and demonstrate comprehension of a variety of literary genres.	✓ ✓	✓	

Goal (skill I will work on)
Describe character development, plot and resolution.

Action Plan (How I will improve)
Re-read the passage and read it slower.

Teacher's Comments: _____

Parent's Signature _____   Teacher's Signature _Sra. Hernandez_
                                                        Ms Beaty

Figure 5.7 Carrie Southerland's reading skill list.

terms her own accomplishments, to reflect on her own learning using this evidence, and to set new goals for herself. Without the pivotal portfolio it would have been much more difficult for me as teacher to get to know my students and to report confidently to their parents about their progress.

Using Reading Assessments to Promote Reading in Two Languages

Rebecca Flint is a visual and kinesthetic learner. She lives with both parents and is the youngest child. She is very social both in and out of school. She likes to communicate both in English and in Spanish, although English is definitely her dominant language. Rebecca is still learning Spanish as a second language. When she started fifth grade, she was very limited in her Spanish oral language. Gradually, during the morning class meetings, she has been able to communicate her ideas clearly and accurately.

Rebecca's reading abilities in English and Spanish have been monitored since kindergarten, using several different reading assessments and inventories. In kindergarten and first grade, Rebecca's teachers used the School District 54 Bilingual Reading Proficiency matrix to evaluate her reading proficiency. This is an informal tool designed to be aligned with the state reading matrix and adjusted to second language learners. Beginning in second grade, Rebecca started to take the formal reading test of the IPT-Spanish. Beginning in third grade, the individual reading inventories (IRIs) were administered. The Qualitative Reading Inventory-3 (Leslie & Caldwell, 2001) is used to assess student's reading abilities in English, and the Spanish version of the Flynt-Cooter reading inventory (Flynt & Cooter, 1998) is used for Spanish reading. As teachers became more familiar with using individual reading inventories, it was felt that the district's bilingual reading proficiency matrix was no longer needed as it provided general information already included in the IRI. Table 5.2 summarizes Rebecca's reading abilities as measured by multiple assessments over her six-year participation in the dual language program.

I recall here that Rebecca Flint is a native English speaker learning Spanish as a second language. The reading portion of the IPT test in Spanish shows that Rebecca grew from a non-Spanish reader in second grade to a competent Spanish reader in fifth grade, according this criteria-based assessment. However, according to the Flynt Cooter Reading Inventory (Flynt & Cooter, 1998), at the end of fifth grade Rebecca is still reading independently only at the third-grade level.

The QRI scores reflect growth in English reading over time as well, as she was reading at a second-grade independent level when she was in third grade, and then she progressed to a fifth-grade independent level at the beginning of fifth grade. Throughout the year, as the teacher, I have to take into consideration data acquired from multiple sources in order to make instructional decisions. My goal is to help Rebecca read at least one grade level higher than she is currently reading in both her first and second language.

I try to provide many rich experiences in reading through a combination of read-aloud, shared reading, and various independent and guided reading experiences for my students. The students in my classroom will not all have exactly the same scores or read at the same level. Our multiple common reading assessments help me to differentiate my students'

Table 5.2 Rebecca's History of Reading Development Using Multiple Assessments

	School District 54 Reading Proficiency Matrix	Idea Proficiency Test (IPT) Reading in Spanish	Flint Cooter Spanish Reading Inventory	Qualitative Reading Inventory for English Reading
K	(2.0) Emergent Spanish Reader			
1st grade	(2.7) Emergent Spanish Reader			
2nd grade	(3.5) Developing Spanish Reader	(12) Non-Spanish Reader		
3rd grade		(23) Non-Spanish Reader		2nd-grade independent
4th grade		(29) Limited Spanish Reader		4th-grade independent
5th grade		(40) Competent Spanish Reader	Beginning of 5th grade: 2nd-grade independent End of 5th grade: 3rd-grade independent	Beginning of 5th grade: 5th-grade independent End of 5th grade: 6th-grade independent

reading abilities in their first language in comparison to their second. They also help me make sound diagnoses about my students' needs in reading in each language and implement differentiated instruction accordingly.

At our school, we use leveled texts to provide students the experience of reading at their independent levels. For example, Rebecca was reading independently at the fifth-grade level in English at the beginning of her fifth grade. This means that Rebecca has strong oral language skills in English, is an accomplished reader in her first language, and has comprehension strategies in place sufficient to understand a variety of texts in English at grade level. For her independent reading, Rebecca is encouraged to read texts that are at her independent reading level (fifth grade). For her

English reading, at the beginning of the year, I put Rebecca in a guided reading group with students who were reading at the fifth-grade independent level. By the end of the year, she is with a group of students who are reading at the sixth-grade independent level.

Rebecca's Spanish reading, however, is much more limited. According to Rebecca's IPT scores in Spanish, she was a limited Spanish reader at the end of fourth grade. According to the Flynt Cooter reading inventory, she was reading independently at a second-grade level in Spanish at the beginning of fifth grade.

Rebecca appears to be an accomplished reader in her first language and reading at grade level, yet she is reading three grade levels below in her second language. I deduce that her lagging Spanish reading level is not caused by a lack of comprehension strategies common in early, novice native language readers. I suspect that it is rather due to her lack of vocabulary and oral language proficiency in Spanish. The instructional decision taken in Rebecca's case was to provide many opportunities for her to engage in various guided reading groups at her instructional level, in this case third grade. During her guided reading instruction, the focus was predominantly on building vocabulary in Spanish.

During guided reading group time with Rebecca's group, I used the story Necesitamos los Insectos, *by Anna Prokos, to teach students a strategy to "preview and predict" vocabulary. We previewed the vocabulary by completing a word sort. Students worked with a partner in their small group to predict how they could sort the words. This strategy was completed before we read the text. As we were reading the text we would highlight the words and discuss them, sometimes by drawing a picture of the word, thinking of examples and non-examples, or acting it out. At the end of the reading we went back to our original word sorts and made changes.*

Another instructional strategy that I taught to Rebecca's group on a different occasion is called "connect two," used to identify and explain connections among key terms. In addition to sorting vocabulary, the students need to connect two terms and explain their reasoning for putting them together. Students in Rebecca's guided reading groups were often actively reading the text and learning a lot of content vocabulary. In addition to building vocabulary, we also worked on having the students actively read by making inferences, predictions, connections, and summaries, or by analyzing character development, author's theme, mood, and style. Students use reading response logs to practice these skills. A sample list of ideas I give my students to aid them in writing reading response logs is included in Figure 5.8.

It made me think that . . .	I don't believe that what happened in this story could happen in real life because . . .
I like the way that . . .	Compare the main character with yourself . . .
I can't believe that . . .	Compare the setting of the story with where you live . . .
I noticed that . . .	How would you resolve the problem in the story . . .
I think that . . .	The main character is like . . . because . . .
I am not sure that . . .	Identify which parts of the text could happen in real life and which parts couldn't . . .
My favorite character is . . . I like how the author . . . I felt sad when . . .	Have you read other books like this? What personal connections can you make? Make a prediction, what would happen if . . . ?
If I were the main character . . .	Create a new person or event . . . How would that change the story?
I think that the theme of this story is . . .	Imagine that the story continues . . . What happens next and why?
The author's narrative style is . . .	Do you believe that the story could have ended differently? How?
Some connections that I make are . . .	How did the main character develop or change?
While I was reading the book I thought that . . .	Do you believe that the main character made the right decisions? Why or why not?
The tone of the book is . . .	Which person was the most important and why?
Something interesting that I learned is . . .	
While I was reading I had the following questions . . .	
I think that the main person and I are similar because . . .	

Figure 5.8   Ideas for responding to literature (translated from Spanish).

It is important not only to match students in a guided reading group but also to match them with books at their independent reading level. Students need to be reading books that are interesting to them and at a level that is not frustrating. I realize that having Rebecca read books in Spanish that are at a fifth- or sixth-grade level when she only reads independently at the second-grade level is not going to help her advance in her reading abilities in Spanish. She does get exposure to text at the fifth-grade level during my read-aloud sessions and during our shared reading experiences. For her independent reading, I coached Rebecca in selecting books that do not frustrate her as a second-language reader of Spanish. Some of the stories that Rebecca read that were at the second-grade independent level were El Sombrero de Tío Nacho, *by Harriet Rohmer,* La Pajarita de Papel, *by Fernando Alonso,* La Sapita Sabia, *by Rosario Ferrre,* El Niño de Cabeza, *by Juan Felipe Herrera,* El Señor Viento Norte, *by Carmen de Posadas,* Billy Mills, *by Lee S. Justice,* Harriet Tubman: Una Lección de Coraje, *by Elizabeth Kernan, and* Necesitamos los Insectos, *by Anna Prokos.*

In addition to using the common formal assessments such as the QRI and the IPT, it is equally important to have ongoing, informal assessments of students' reading on a daily basis. I use a reading conference log to make running records of each student's reading during our conferences. This information allows me to learn more about strategies they use and find ways to help them read more effectively. During a reading conference, I might ask them to read aloud for me, share something special about their story, or do a retelling to see how well they understand the story. I also give students my assessment of their reading and give them constructive feedback and suggestions on how to improve a particular reading skill.

I ask students to write reading responses to tell me what they like about the story or what they thought of the new information they learn from their reading. Students' responses to their own reading are another way that I can informally assess their comprehension.

Informal classroom-based assessments that I implement in my daily teaching are very powerful in that they guide me in my planning for instruction. When I look for great stories to read during read-aloud sessions or shared reading and when I plan lessons for guided reading groups, I rely on the information gained from these assessments to guide my decisions when guiding students individually and planning group instruction.

Most important, as in the case of Rebecca the use of information gained from multiple sources of assessment has helped me differentiate reading instruction for individual students. I was able to assign appropriate guided reading groups in English and Spanish to Rebecca, and I was able to guide her in selecting appropriate leveled books for her reading in both languages. As a result, by the end of her fifth-grade year, Rebecca has gained one grade level of reading proficiency in both her first and second language, meeting my learning goal for her.

Evidence-Based Program and Professional Development

Mrs. Danette Myer, the School District 54 dual language program coordinator, provided the following response when asked how she uses multiple sources of data to (1) guide teachers in their instructional decisions, (2) provide needed staff development to increase teachers' effectiveness, and (3) effect program changes as a result of student assessment.

The student pivotal portfolio is an important means for teachers and administrators to discuss individual student progress and group goals. As students transition from one grade to the next, teachers are able to share how a child has grown and challenges he or she continues to have. Because this discussion occurs with accompanying work samples and rubrics, it is much richer than a conversation that includes only the current teacher's perceptions and ideas. The teacher who will have the student the following year can actively assess and question, since the samples are present available during the conversation.

    This is also useful when students who are considered ELLs when entering the program develop enough English proficiency to be formally considered fluent English speakers, readers, and writers. During the ELL transition conference between dual language teachers and me, classroom and large-scale assessment data are reviewed to ensure that the student is indeed proficient and is not longer in need of English as a second language services, as mandated by the state, even though the student will continue to participate in the dual language program by choice. By examining the evidence included in the student's pivotal portfolio, we can collaboratively make the final decision as to whether or not the student can change his or her ELL status. Although this change of status does not affect the instruction already available through the dual language program, it does have an effect in the ELL accountability formula that the state uses to evaluate and fund TBE programs.

The portfolio data are also useful for determining instructional plans for groups of students. Erminda Garcia, a first-grade teacher and teacher trainer from California, has used results from rubrics and checklists to create scattergrams of student performance. These scattergrams can then be used to plan for small group instruction that meets the common needs of particular students. The dual language teachers in School District 54 have begun to experiment with this type of data analysis, using data gained from various existing common assessments. Staff development was spent to introduce this practice, and plans were made to further improve teacher's abilities in using the scattergrams.

Some of the portfolio data are also used by the district to determine placement in the summer reading program. The purpose of the program is to aid students who have developed oral proficiency in English but are not developing as quickly as expected in English reading. Teachers recommend students who met this criterion, along with evidence of their oral proficiency and reading achievement from SOPR, IPT, and QRI results. Because these are common assessments used in the program, teachers always have assessment data for their students on hand when they need to complete a recommendation for summer school or need information over time for a pre-referral meeting with the child study team. This information aids in choosing qualifying students and also in forming instructional groups within the summer program that are based on student needs.

The pivotal portfolio is also a tool for program improvement. Teachers across schools who teach the same grade level use common portfolio assessments to compare how students are doing in particular areas and discuss instructional strategies that led to success with different students. For example, in reviewing recent data from the IPT and SOPR, it has become clear to us that older-grade students need more targeted instruction in developing higher levels of oral proficiency. This is especially true of the native Japanese-speaking students in English and the native English-speaking students in Spanish. Without the data, teacher assessment of oral proficiency would be merely anecdotal. This information will be used to help teachers plan activities that develop higher oral proficiency for these students. Plans are also made for further training in oral proficiency interviews to help teachers better assess student second-language proficiency when a formal test is not available in the target language.

At the same, teachers realized that we needed to have a better tool to assess the language proficiency growth of native English-speaking students learning Japanese, since there was no commercial instrument available. During the summer of 2004, dual language teachers worked on a Japanese language proficiency checklist to help teachers informally monitor their students' progress in Japanese as a Second Language (JSL) from year to year. They sought guidance from expert second-language educators during the Center for Advanced Research on Language Acquisition (CARLA) summer institute on assessment, and sought responses from colleagues in the Japanese immersion program in the Portland schools before implementing it in the fall of 2005. The structure of the pivotal portfolio made us realize what assessment was missing for a particular group of students and helped us follow rigorous standards when we had to make our own common assessment for program use.

As a facilitator, I constantly rely on assessments in the pivotal portfolio when discussing student progress with dual language teachers. Because we have a set of common assessments, it is expected that results from these assessments will be shared as part of the evidence discussed when evaluating and considering the needs of particular students. And because common assessments are implemented at each grade level and at consistent time intervals, the portfolio provides invaluable historical data about the student's progress as a learner over time in multiple content subjects in both languages. Dual language teachers have come to rely on the student portfolio as a way to get to know their students at the beginning of the year.

Since the portfolio construct is flexible, from year to year the teachers and I meet to review the content of the portfolio and add or eliminate assessments based on new accountability demands or program changes. Often, these conversations result in teacher-selected staff development that is needed to improve our program.

The rich data from multiple assessments have also been useful when I need to report to parents and the community on the status of dual language students' progress. Although state tests results are always included in the report, formative assessments and sample student work have helped to paint a balanced picture of both growth and achievements of students. By the same token, the formative assessment adds to our program evaluation and provides us with another alternative means of gauging program effectiveness based on authentic student products. We constantly have to advocate for the dual language program and the belief that bilingualism and biliteracy are beneficial for all students.

Using the graph in Figure 5.9 to compare the native English speakers and native Spanish speakers in the dual language program with the per-

formance of students at the district and state level in English, we can advocate for the continuation or expansion of the program. Third-grade scores for our native Spanish-speaking students are historically lower since they have not had adequate time to develop enough English to be successful on an all-English test. This often leads teachers and principals as well as district personnel to doubt the efficacy of the program and begin discussing using more English with students.

Figure 5.9 illustrates that once students have had the sufficient five to seven years necessary for their language abilities to develop in English, they are on par with their non-ELL peers. In fact, many exceed state standards. This longitudinal view of summative data demonstrates that, given adequate time for growth, ELLs from well-implemented dual language programs achieve high academic results in English.

At the local level, in addition to state achievement tests in English, we can use the formative assessments and sample student work to paint a balanced picture of both growth and achievements of students in Spanish or Japanese also. We need to be true to our goals of bilingualism and biliteracy rather than just English performance. We know that if we do not use and share assessments in other languages, our students, staff, and parents may begin to devalue that achievement. Similarly, the formative assess-

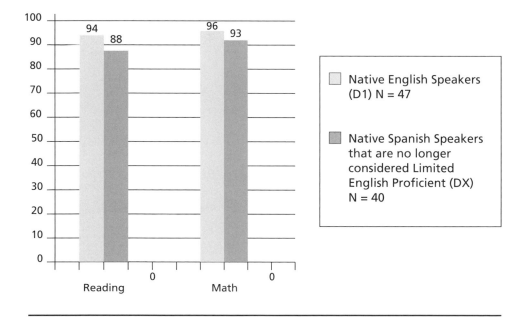

Figure 5.9 ISAT scores for students in the Spanish-English dual language program, grades 4 through 6, at MacArthur and Enders-Salk schools in Schaumberg School District 54.

ment adds to our program evaluation and provides us with another alternative means of gauging program effectiveness based on authentic student products.

Summative data, coupled with formative assessment, can be triangulated to validate developmental bilingual programs and rally common political will to pursue best practices in bilingual education in local communities. In addition, such data add to the national dialogue on second-language education by providing substantial evidence to promote additive bilingualism.

Conclusion

This chapter has explored how a dual language teacher and dual language program coordinator use evidence to drive decision making in School District 54's dual language program. As shown through one dual language teacher's testimony, the information gained from the variety of common assessments in the pivotal portfolio is used at the classroom level to:

- Differentiate instruction for individual students

- Diagnose individual students' strengths and weakness

- Group students appropriately for instructional purposes

- Inform daily lesson planning and implementation

- Help teachers get to know their students as diverse and complicated learners

- Give students timely feedback to improve learning

- Provide students with tools for self-assessment and reflection

- Communicate to parents students' progress, using multiple sources of information and authentic student work samples

- Guide students in setting realistic but challenging individual goals

- Provide both teachers and students with common, well-established criteria for evaluation

- Keep both teachers and students mutually accountable for teaching and learning

At the program level, the same information is used by the dual language coordinator to:

- Discuss students' progress with teachers and help them make instructional decisions based on evidence of learning

- Coach new teachers to problem solve instructional concerns about their students

- Provide groups of teachers with student performance as evidence to support arguments for changes in instructional practices

- Collaborate in constructing formative assessment for students when needed while using high standards to drive the design

- Evaluate the effectiveness of the program and make community reports

The evidence that School District 54 educators collaboratively collect, analyze, and use clearly serves a wide range of purposes. As Mrs. Meyers emphasizes at the end of her discussion, in these contentious times in the field of bilingual education, we desperately need evidence of what students can realistically be expected to achieve academically in a second language at different moments in time and over time. Educators can then use this evidence of actual student growth and achievement to demonstrate the effectiveness of well-implemented dual language education and to argue for policies that are based on evidence, not ideology.

Questions for Reflection and Action

1. As you read about the students in Mrs. Hernandez' classroom and how she uses assessment information to guide her students' learning, recall and reflect upon your own assessment practices. List all the current purposes of assessment in your classroom and compare them with Mrs. Hernandez's. What similarities and differences do you see?

2. Identify five strategies that you learned from Mrs. Hernandez and Mrs. Meyer that can be applied to your own setting? What changes might you make?

Using Evidence to Drive Decision Making in Transitional Bilingual Programs

Chapter Overview

In this chapter, two teachers in a transitional bilingual education program, Mrs. Naseem Alibhai and Mrs. Magali Williams, share their experiences using information gleaned from students' pivotal portfolios to differentiate instruction for students and help them transition successfully into the English dominant school environment. In addition, Mrs. Wojtysiak, the bilingual program coordinator, discusses how she uses the pivotal portfolio as a source of information to discuss students' progress with teachers and improve program services.

Guiding Questions

- How can a teacher use information from common assessments to differentiate instruction for individual bilingual students in their classrooms?
- How can teachers use the same data to communicate and collaborate with each other across categorical programs about students they share?
- What are the advantages of using information from common assessments to guide professional development and program improvement?

Key Concepts:

- The pivotal portfolio helps teachers use data from common assessments when discussing students' progress and making collaborative instructional plans.
- The pivotal portfolio provides teachers with rich details of each student's growth over time, thus helping teachers to differentiate instruction for English language learners more effectively.
- At the program level, assessment information gleaned from students' portfolio provides authentic and rich evidence of students' learning to guide program improvement.

This chapter recounts how educators use assessment data to make instructional decisions and guide learning in the transitional bilingual program (TBE) in the Schaumburg School District 54. The teachers included are a Hindi-English bilingual teacher, Mrs. Naseem Alibhai, and a Spanish-English bilingual teacher, Mrs. Magali Williams, both of whom work in TBE resource classrooms. They share stories and strategies of how they use evidence of student learning to help them differentiate instruction for high-achieving as well as struggling English language learners (ELLs), and how they use the common assessments in the pivotal portfolio to make decisions about students' readiness to exit the TBE program. The TBE program coordinator, Mrs. Barbara Wojtysiak, then describes how assessment information plays an influential role in her work as a staff developer and a program coordinator. We use the real names of Mrs. Alibhai, Mrs. Williams, and Mrs. Wojtysiak with their permission, and we use pseudonyms for the students they discuss.

The educators' accounts provide practical illustrations of how they collect different types of assessment data, turn the data into useful information or evidence, and take instructional action based on that evidence. This chapter features the strategic uses of the information systematically gathered in the pivotal portfolio by teachers in the TBE program as they work to provide appropriate, differentiated instruction to their diverse ELLs. It illustrates how educators can use multiple common assessments to provide authentic evidence of student learning, guide staff development, and improve the program. The chapter also highlights the collaborative nature of decision making by educators in School District 54.

Assessment for Learning: Mrs. Alibhai's and Mrs. Williams's Practice

School District 54 has a comprehensive, gradual-exit, K–8 transitional bilingual program (TBE) that serves ELLs in self-contained and resource classrooms. The three major components of the TBE program are ESL instruction, native language support for academic content learning, and assistance in the cultural transition into the general education setting. In the primary grades, students in self-contained TBE classes develop native language literacy as they simultaneously acquire English. For example, most native Spanish-speaking ELLs are taught formal Spanish literacy from kindergarten to second grade, at which point English literacy begins to be taught formally. At the upper grade levels, ELLs are integrated into general education classes for part of the day and receive ESL instruction and native language support from a bilingual teacher and bilingual assistants for the rest of the day. Services are gradually reduced as students gain the English language proficiency they need to participate and achieve in the all-English classroom.

As a first example, Naseem Alibhai describes how she used evidence to make instructional decisions about two of her ELLs. Mrs. Alibhai is a bilingual elementary school resource teacher who speaks several languages, including Gujurati, Hindi, Urdu, and English. She teaches ELLs from first through sixth grades. Although the majority of her students are native Gujurati or Hindi speakers, she also serves other ELLs who speak other native languages. Mrs. Alibhai works with a bilingual assistant, Mrs. Shah, who is fluent in Urdu and English. Mrs. Alibhai describes how she used reading and writing data to argue for additional learning supports for Maha Fardha, a first-grade ELL whose home language is Urdu. For another student, Radhay Parikh, a third-grade ELL who speaks Gujarati at home, she used the pivotal portfolio as a tool for collaboration with mainstream teachers to evaluate Radhay's progress. As a result of this evaluation, Radhay was able to participate in the gifted education program at the school. Mrs. Alibhai then used multiple criteria to determine that Radhay was ready to exit the TBE program.

We then turn to the experiences of Magali Williams. Mrs. Williams is a bilingual elementary school resource teacher who speaks Spanish and English. She teaches ELLs from grades 1 through 6. Although most of her students speak Spanish, Mrs. Williams also serves students from other language backgrounds who have chosen to attend this particular school as their school of choice in School District 54. In addition to teaching ESL, Mrs. Williams teaches early literacy in Spanish to ELLs who are native Spanish speakers before transitioning them to English literacy. Mrs. Williams first describes how she used multiple sources of information to determine that Carlitos Morales, a second-grade native Spanish-speaking ELL, was ready to begin formal literacy instruction in English. Then Mrs. Williams shares how she determined that José Sandoval, a native Spanish speaker, qualified for special education services in conjunction with TBE services.

Using Reading and Writing Data to Argue for Additional Learning Supports

Mrs. Alibhai describes how she used evidence about one ELL's reading abilities to determine the need for a reading intervention program.

Maha Fardha is a first-grade ELL from the southwestern region of India. She speaks Urdu at home with her family. She is the youngest child. When she first came to the United States with her family, she knew only a few words in English. She was assessed for the TBE program when she registered at Armstrong School in 2004 and qualified for placement in the program. Her parents accepted the recommendation for placement for her and her older brother. Following the model of the TBE program in School District 54, Maha was placed in a general education first-grade homeroom, where she received instruction in math, science, art, music, and physical education. While her English-only classmates were receiving literacy instruction with their homeroom teacher, Maha and other identified ELLs from her class, would come to my TBE resource classroom for ESL and literacy instruction, as well as native language support for other content subjects as needed.

I used various assessment tools to diagnose the areas of need for Maha and also to assess growth in all areas of literacy. The Qualitative Reading Inventory (QRI) was used to assess her word identification skills and her silent and listening reading comprehension. Informal assessment was done through classroom observation, journal review, graphic organizers, and comprehension questions about the stories she read. I also used the TBE program reading and writing matrices and teacher-designed rubrics to monitor the independent level of this student.

The reading assessment results summarized in Table 6.1 point to the fact that Maha was reading at least two grades below grade level. In addition, the results of Maha's most current state-mandated English proficiency test (ACCESS test) gave another indication of her weak reading abilities (Table 6.2). Although her oral proficiency level was strong, her reading and writing abilities were lagging behind. Her ACCESS 2006 results put her on a Tier B designation. Students must reach Tier C or level 5 before being considered English proficient.

These assessment results were supported by my observation of Maha's reading behaviors. I had observed that Maha's oral language skills had increased after she joined our program, although her vocabulary was still

Table 6.1 Results from Maha's Reading Assessments Using the QRI and the District TBE Program Reading Matrix

Assessment	Date	Results
Qualitative Reading Inventory	February 2004	Frustrational at Pre-primer level for word identification and silent reading comprehension
Informal Reading Matrix	October 2003	Pre-reader (stage 1 out of 6)
Informal Reading Matrix	April 2004	Emergent Reader (stage 2 out of 6)
Informal Reading Matrix	October 2004	Emergent Reader (stage 2 out of 6)

limited. She could read a word on one page but not recognize it on the next page. She showed slow, labored, inaccurate reading of single words in isolation. Maha reads word by word, trying to decipher the letter sounds that form the words. Consequently, her comprehension is limited. She finds it challenging to express herself in writing in complete meaningful sentences. She misreads, omits, or even adds small function words, such as an, a, from, the, to, were, are, of.

My anecdotal records of observation, coupled with results from multiple assessments, had led me to believe that Maha was a candidate for our summer reading intervention program for ELLs. I used all these data to make a recommendation for her to participate in the summer reading intervention program.

Maha was accepted based on the QRI scores I provided and her home-room teachers' and my recommendations. The use of multiple assessment sources helps me gauge my student's needs, and it provides me with ample evidence to recommend students for participation in a program that will help to improve their reading abilities.

Table 6.2 Maha's ACCESS 2006 Scores

Listening	Speaking	Reading	Writing	Composite
4.1	6.0	3.7	3.5	3.9

Using the Pivotal Portfolio to Collaborate with General and Special Education Teachers

Mrs. Alibhai collaborated with another teacher in recommending one of her ELL students, Radhay, for the gifted education program.

Radhay Parikh is a third-grade ELL student. Radhay's family comes from India, but he was born in the United States. He and his family speak Gujarati at home. When his family registered him for kindergarten in our district, he qualified for placement in the TBE program. He attended the half-day kindergarten program in the classroom taught by a bilingual teacher who spoke English and Gujarati. In first through third grade, he continued to receive bilingual services through the TBE resource program, being assigned to a general education homeroom and going to the TBE resource classroom for ESL, literacy instruction, and native language support in other content subjects. I was Radhay's bilingual teacher since first grade.

Radhay has always been a well-behaved, polite, and inquisitive student. His parents are involved in his schooling, helping him with his homework, attending parent conferences, and assisting at school functions and parents nights.

As a teacher, I believe it is my duty to find ways to challenge my students every day to do their best and to find opportunities for them to excel in their learning. Radhay caught my attention because of his special abilities. I saw traits of giftedness in Radhay when he was in second grade, especially in math reasoning. Even though he was still learning English as a second language, he solved math problems with ease and often came up with alternative solutions as well.

Radhay's performance in math transferred to his other academic activities. He was very focused in any learning activity he was involved in. He seemed more mature in many ways than his age peers and older students. I tried to challenge Radhay in my classroom by having him teach students once he had completed his own work. He would come up with brilliant answers that very few second graders would be capable of.

I usually discuss students' behavior and performances with their homeroom teachers on a regular basis. During these discussions, his teacher and I talked about Radhay's alertness and participation in class. As his English proficiency grew in the domains of speaking, reading and writing, as evidenced through his bilingual portfolio, we agreed to gradually transition Radhay into the English-only environment by having him spend less time in the bilingual resource classroom and more time in the general education classroom. The bilingual individual instructional plan (BIIP; see Chapter 1) provided a framework to discuss Radhay's growth in conversations with his homeroom teacher. Using the BIIP, we were able to correlate Radhay's English proficiency level based on assessment with his academic functioning, as observed and evaluated by his homeroom teacher, to plan how much time Radhay should spend in the all-English homeroom and when he should attend my bilingual class to learn ESL and receive bilingual instructional support. The result is a collaboratively negotiated plan to gradually help Radhay transition into the English-only classroom while ensuring his academic success.

By reviewing the plan with his teacher at each grading period, we work as a team to make good instructional decisions for Radhay, based on common assessments and his daily work in both of his learning environments at school. As a result of these discussions, and after reviewing Radhay's outstanding performance in both classrooms despite his still growing English proficiency, we agreed to recommend Radhay for placement in the gifted education program in the winter of 2005. This decision is quite exceptional, as few ELLs are considered for the gifted education program in our district. Most of the tests used for gifted education screening are English achievement tests and therefore are quite challenging to ELLs, who have to meet stringent qualifying criteria. However, we believed that Radhay's pivotal portfolio and our observation of his classroom performances provided strong evidence to make a case for his giftedness.

As we discussed with Radhay's parents our ideas at our parent-teacher conference, they were delighted and showed strong interest in having Radhay apply to participate in the gifted education program. His homeroom teacher and I together completed the teacher's recommendation form for gifted testing, using many of our observations as well as samples of Radhay's work as evidence to include in our recommendations. He was subsequently tested (using the Terra Nova test and other cognitive test batteries) and qualified for gifted services. The gifted resource teacher began providing services to him in the fall of 2005. Radhay has since excelled in the gifted education program.

I believe that the giftedness in Radhay is undeniable, but we cannot ignore his parents' involvement in his educational journey. Both his parents are very supportive and provide as many resources as they can. His father asked me how I teach students to write in different genres because he wanted to help his son practice at home. He told me that he was taking this opportunity as a challenge to help Radhay improve his writing skills, as that was the last area of improvement Radhay needed to meet all criteria for exiting the bilingual program.

Using Multiple Criteria to Determine ELLs' Readiness to Exit the Program

Different assessment tools were used to ascertain that Radhay was ready to exit the bilingual program. The Qualitative Reading Inventory (Leslie & Caldwell, 2001) was used to assess his word identification skills and silent and listening reading comprehension. Informal assessment was done through classroom observation, journal review, graphic organizers, and comprehension questions about the story read. Reading and writing matrices and rubrics were also used to monitor and determine the functioning level of this student. He scored high on speaking, reading, and writing assessments.

I met with Radhay's homeroom teacher to discuss Radhay's performance and attitude in class. According to her, Radhay had strong computation skills and applied that knowledge to new mathematical concepts. He learned new concepts at a pace above monolingual English-speaking students. After our discussion, the homeroom teacher completed a recommendation form that included her evaluation of Radhay's performance in all core content subjects, as well as his work samples, which were included as evidence to show that Radhay was ready to transition out of the bilingual program. Her recommendation for Radhay to exit the TBE program was quite strong. She included Radhay's latest essays as evidence of his English writing abilities. The essays that he wrote displayed clear focus, organization, and appropriate conventions.

After I secured the recommendation from the homeroom teacher, I reviewed Radhay's pivotal portfolio once more to make sure we had all the assessment data necessary to show his readiness to exit the program, based on our program criteria for exit (discussed in Chapter 4).

Using our cumulative record form (see Worksheet 15 in the Appendix) as a summarizing tool, I met with the program coordinator and presented her with evidence that Radhay had met all criteria for exit from the TBE program. We reviewed the evidence and together made the decision that Radhay could exit our program. The decision was made based on information gained from all pertinent assessments, including classroom-based assessment and teacher recommendations, program-based common assessment, current samples of the student's work, and summative standardized test results. Table 6.3 summarizes the assessment results included in his portfolio.

Table 6.3 Radhay's Assessment History Using Multiple Common Assessments

Oral Proficiency Assessments

Grade	IPT	SOPR
Kindergarten	Level C—Limited English	3s and 4s (out of 5)
1st grade	Level D—Limited English	All 4s
2nd grade	Level F—Fluent English	4s and 5s
3rd grade	Level F—Fluent English	All 5s

Reading Proficiency Assessments

Grade	IPT Reading	SD54 Reading Matrix	Qualitative Reading Inventory
Kindergarten	35/46—Beginning	Pre-reader/Novice	Not available
1st grade	59/61—Early	Novice/Competent	Pre-primer (Independent Level)
2nd grade	42/51—Competent	Competent/Advanced	Level 1 (Independent Level)
3rd grade	Not administered	Advanced	Levels 3 and 4 (Independent Level)

Writing Proficiency Assessments

Grade	IPT Writing	SD 54 Writing Matrix
Kindergarten	13/15—Beginning	
1st grade	18/21—Beginning	
2nd grade	16/19—Limited	3s and 4s (out of 6)
3rd grade	Not administered	5s and 6s (out of 6)

Other Standardized Assessments

Grade	ACCESS for ELLs	Terra Nova
2nd grade		R—44%ile, Lang—38%ile
3rd grade	L—6.0, S—5.7, R—4.8, W—3.8 Composite Score—4.8	

Because he met all the criteria for exiting, Radhay transitioned out of the TBE program in April 2006. Now, Radhay comes to my class during lunch to participate in a voluntary Hindi literacy class that I teach to students who are speakers of Hindi but lack literacy skills. I believe that Radhay's success is partly aided by the fact that we, as collaborative teachers and administrators, have tools inherent in our program assessment framework (such as the BIIP and common assessments of the pivotal portfolio) to help us use multiple assessment data and make collaborative decisions on behalf of our ELL students.

Using Evidence to Motivate the Transition from Spanish to English Literacy Instruction

Mrs. Williams relates how she used multiple forms of assessment data to determine that Carlitos Morales was ready for English literacy instruction.

Carlitos Morales is a second grader who was designated a limited English speaker and a beginning English reader and writer on the basis of the IDEA Proficiency Test (IPT) test results, taken in January 2005. He is very social and verbal. His older brother and sisters have been in the bilingual program in the district. Although Carlitos was identified as a limited English speaker, he has good command of his basic interpersonal communication skills, (BICS) while his cognitive academic language proficiency (CALP) is developing. He reads at grade level in his native language, which is Spanish. The terms basic interpersonal communication skills and cognitive academic language proficiency were coined in the 1980s by Jim Cummins, who found that ELLs develop their social, informal language proficiency first and that it may take up to seven year for them to develop adequate academic language proficiency in their second language. Carlitos has been in the general education classroom since first grade for math, science, and social studies, with support from a Spanish-speaking bilingual instructional assistant for math. He performs at grade level in math and has a strong understanding of concepts and skills. When Carlitos was given the Illlinois State Early Literacy (ISEL) test in Spanish in the spring of first grade, he demonstrated abilities comparable to those of a child at the beginning of the second grade. Based on this assessment, I knew he had a strong foundation in his first language.

In English, he reads independently at grade 1 level on the QRI Word

ID test. I notice that Carlitos is able to fluently read all of the language experience activities that I implement in the classroom. The activities include first- and second-grade high-frequency words. He has no difficulty identifying high-frequency words that he has been exposed to in the classroom. He has a growing love for words and has demonstrated great interest in reading English books.

Carlitos has also gained fluency in English by reading weekly poems in English in his bilingual classroom, as well as in his general education classroom. The students read the same poem in a group for about two weeks and then they perform the poem for the class. He is gaining confidence in his abilities. The poems are chosen by themes or topics they are studying in their content area ESL or science and social studies class.

Another sign that Carlitos is ready for English literacy is that he has also begun to choose to write in English on his own, without teacher initiating or prompting. He is also asking to read books from the English baskets of leveled readers on his own.

When I gave him the ISEL in English, here are Carlitos's results from that assessment. His scores on word recognition were 20/22; he read the selected passage at a 93% accuracy rate, with 88 wcpm; and he correctly identified 12 of 14 vocabulary words. His spelling score was 2/10 and his comprehension score was 5/12.

Although Carlitos's spelling and comprehension scores were not high, based on my observation of his strong ability in Spanish reading, his quick acquisition and retention of new English vocabulary, and how he has shown great interest in English in the classroom, I am confident that Carlitos is ready to try to transition into more English reading.

Table 6.4 summarizes the informal reading inventories that I used to assess Carlitos's early reading abilities in Spanish and in English. My informal observations as well as the reading assessments give me information and insight as to when to transition the student into English literacy. Carlitos's behaviors in my classroom as a reader and an ELL student, coupled with evidence from the assessment results, have given me every indication that he is ready to begin the transition into English literacy.

Readiness is an important factor I consider before I begin to transition a student from Spanish into English literacy because I want this decision to be a smooth, child-centered, and student-directed transition for Carlitos. Although I trust myself to make the best decision for my students based on my daily observation of their performances in my class, I am glad that I have many assessments available to me as a teacher to help confirm my observation and evaluation of my students' progress.

Table 6.4 Carlitos's IRI Results in His First and Second Languages, Using Various Individual Reading Inventories

Date	Inventory	Language	Results
9/04 (grade 1)	ISEL	Spanish	Alphabet 42/54 Comprehension 13/21 Initial sound 7/10 Word naming 5/9 Letter sounds 14/25 Word recognition 0/22
8/05 (grade 2)	ISEL	Spanish	No Spanish ISEL Grade 2
5/06 (grade 2)	ISEL	English	Spelling 2/10 Word recognition 20/22 Fluency 88 wcpm Passage comprehension 93% Comprehension 5/12 Extended response 10/36 Vocabulary 12/14
5/06 (grade 2)	QRI	English	Word ID: Instructional—Grade 2 Listen. Comp.: Instr.—Primer Silent Rdg.: Instr.—Primer

Using Multiple Assessments to Determine ELLs' Special Education Needs

In this section, Mrs. Williams explains how she used multiple sources of data to recommend one of her ELLs for special education services.

José Sandoval is a third-grade student in a multiage third-grade and fourth-grade classroom. He was born in the United States and so is representive of a growing number of the Spanish-speaking bilingual population. The first language that he spoke, according to his mother, was English. At the age of four, José went to live with his grandmother in Mexico. He attended kindergarten and part of first grade there. When he returned to the United States, he was placed in a monolingual English general education classroom. His mother stated that he did not need bilingual services. He is an only child and lives with his mother, aunt, and two cousins.

José's first-grade teacher expressed some concerns about his lack of progress in her class. She requested a screening of José's English proficiency. The screening consisted of an English proficiency test in speaking, listening, reading, and writing. According to the parameters of the test, Jose qualified for placement in the TBE program. A recommendation was then made to José's mother, and she agreed that he should receive services in the TBE program. José received native language literacy and content-based ESL instruction from the bilingual resource teacher through the district's TBE resource program model. Math, science, and social studies instruction was delivered in the monolingual general education classroom.

When Jose entered second grade, in addition to receiving Spanish literacy instruction in my class, he was placed in an English+ classroom and received instruction in other subjects from his second-grade teacher, who is also bilingual. The English+ classroom is unique to School District 54. Started in 1998, it is a general education classroom where the teacher is bilingual and speaks the home language of the ELLs in her class. Consequently, this general education teacher can provide native language support when necessary to ELLs in her own classroom. ELL students in these classes benefit in that they are integrated in a self-contained classroom with other native English-speaking students and yet they have a bilingual teacher as their instructor to provide native language support as needed.

At Dirksen School, the English+ teacher and I have adjacent classrooms with an adjoining door. This provides us with a great opportunity for communicating and working together. As we observed José, we begin to see some of the same learning behaviors that José exhibited in each of our classes. I observed some of the same learning behaviors in José in Spanish that the E+ teacher saw happening in English in her class.

As we collaborated and shared our observation notes with each other, we realized that José seemed to have problem processing information presented in class. We noticed that the processing issues and behaviors occur in both English and Spanish environments. This led us to suspect that José might have a disability that had gone undetected to that point. As we documented the use of our strategies with José, the modifications that we made in his instruction, and the outcomes, we shared our concerns and José's portfolio with the school psychologist and began the process of referring José for a special education evaluation to the school's child study team.

In second grade, José was a limited English speaker, limited English writer, and a non-English reader, according to the results of the Idea Proficiency Test in English taken in midyear. When José began third grade, his oral fluency was at grade level in English, but he had difficulty comprehending, retelling, recalling important facts and details in his reading, and sequencing events in both English and Spanish.

In January of his third-grade year, José took the QRI. He can read independently only at the first-grade level. I also noticed that José had difficulty applying strategies to understand texts. He did not understand what he has to do to help with his reading. José struggled to complete writing tasks. It was not easy for him to put his thoughts in written form in an organized manner. He had great difficulty following oral and written directions and often took them literally even when various attempts were made to clarify. José also struggled in math. He did not focus during instruction or during work periods. His computation was weak, as are his problem-solving skills. He had trouble with algorithms and multistep computations. He did not perform well on math tasks deaing with measurement, fractions, decimals, or money.

In addition, José had difficulty organizing his ideas and expressing his thoughts in English and Spanish. He struggled to find the correct words to share his thinking, even when prompted. He had difficulty staying on topic when speaking. José seemed to have difficulty with word retrieval.

José was unable to complete a task without constant teacher prompting and cueing. He had difficulty recalling what he had been asked and therefore could not follow through or complete a task independently. When working in a cooperative group, he relied on his peers to guide him through the task. José tried to be very responsible about his work, but his inability to retain information and tasks inhibited him from being as responsible as he wanted to be.

All modifications and accommodations were documented. In third grade, as we shared our information based on our common assessments and our documentation with the school child study team, we were able to convince them to do a case study to screen José for special education services. José was evaluated and qualified for both special education services and speech and language services. Assessing and documenting our modification strategies played a big part in helping the child study team make its decision to qualify José for services.

Using Multiple Assessments to Guide Program-Level Decision Making

Barbara Wojtysiak is the coordinator for the TBE program in School District 54. In this capacity, she is responsible for implementing all language support services for ELLs in the district. Mrs. Wojtysiak meets frequently with principals and teachers to support them in their daily implementation of the program. She also is responsible for submitting state grants and reports related to ELL education. Mrs. Woktysiak writes about how she uses School District 54's assessment framework in her capacity to support instruction, develop effective staff development plans, and make program improvements.

Coaching Teachers to Make Sound Instructional Decisions

As a teacher assesses and observes her students in a TBE program, she knows that it is essential to document the growth of those students in all areas of language development. In this way she is able to adjust her instruction to meet the individual needs of her students. Students who enter programs to develop English language proficiency come from very diverse backgrounds in education, home language development, and school experiences. The approach of the TBE program can not be "one size fits all." The TBE assessment portfolio in School District 54 was developed to address the needs of TBE teachers who have these very diverse students in their classrooms every day.

One of my responsibilities as the TBE program coordinator is to observe the bilingual teachers in their classrooms and discuss with them effective instructional practices. I often serve as a mentor for new teachers and a resource for more experienced teachers in their daily implementation of the program. The pivotal portfolio is the tool that I regularly use to anchor my conversation about students during these meetings. When I visit classrooms, bilingual teachers often want to discuss their concerns about the progress of one or more of their students. The first place we go to is the student's bilingual portfolio with all its cumulative assessments. We look at each language domain separately and discuss the student's progress in speaking, listening, reading, and writing, as well as the length of time in the United States, length of time in the program, and family dynamics and support. For example, in a discussion about Maha, it was important to note that she had been in the United States for three years and was the youngest in her family, and that her parents were not overly concerned about her lack of progress in reading. Her teacher showed me her progress in oral English proficiency using her scores on the IPT, and we spent some time reviewing informal reading inventories, which showed a weakness in word identification and silent reading comprehension.

Using this information that we have gathered from various assessment sources, we developed a plan to document reading interventions that her teacher could use to build word automaticity and silent reading comprehension. During the next several months, this plan also helped support the decision to recommend Maha for participation in the summer reading intervention program and suggest placement into a group with similar instructional needs.

Staff Development Planning and Implementation

The assessment portfolio also gives teachers and administrators a common assessment framework when discussing ELL students' learning. As students move within the district from kindergarten to first grade, from sixth grade to junior high, or at any other times, teachers in our district speak the same data language. When teachers talk about students who are designated as ESL Level I, they all have a similar mental picture of the speaking, reading, and writing proficiencies of those students, based on assessments familiar to them all. TBE portfolios include a set of required common assessments, including summative and formative measures, from which instructional decisions are discussed and collaboratively reached.

It has been important to our department that teachers don't see the bilingual portfolio as just a compilation of assessment results. We have found that staff development time must be spent helping the teachers analyze the data and then leading them to use the data to affect instruction in their classrooms. Over the past seven years of the administration of the IMAGE state assessment, bilingual district office administrators and staff have reviewed the yearly data of designated schools and shared their analyses with school administrators and bilingual teachers. We have added information to the state data, such as the number of years a student has been in our program and a comparison of individual student scores from one year to the next.

This collaboration in the review of data helps us to determine if a student has made adequate progress over the year of participation in our TBE program. We can share this analysis with teachers and their administrators at the school level. I have also found it necessary to provide instructional decision-making support through staff development opportunities after the data have been shared. At these staff development sessions, bilingual teachers bring their rosters of IMAGE results and work in teams to analyze the data to group students for reading instruction and math support, answering critical questions that focus the discussions. Experi-

enced and new teachers alike have benefited from these opportunities to confer with their colleagues, who share the same teaching assignments. During these conversations, teachers discuss the implications of the assessment results for their students in terms of their learning, and how the results reflect the effectiveness of teaching strategies that are used with students. Teachers have opportunities to share with each other what works and collaborate to find solutions for things that do not work in their classrooms. Figure 6.1 shows the cycle of collaboration we use in School District 54 to provide effective staff development in the implementation of the BASIC model of assessment described in this book.

Program Improvement

For the first 20 years of its existence after 1975, the TBE/TPI program in School District 54 was basically a tutoring program. Students brought assigned work from their homeroom teachers to the resource classroom, requesting help and further explanation in completing the assignments from their TBE teachers. Students received ESL instruction through the use of

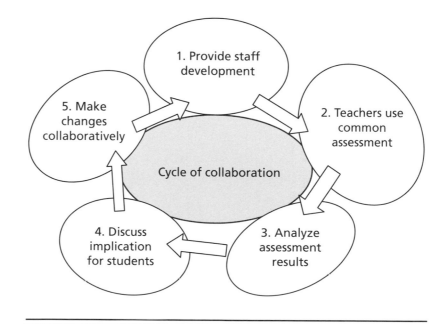

Figure 6.1 Cycle of collaboration among educators in the implementation of the BASIC model.

general education materials, with the resource teacher using core materials at lower grade levels and proceeding at a slower pace.

With the inception of high-stakes testing for ELLs in the late 1990s, it became evident that our TBE/TPI teachers would be held to a higher standard of achievement for their students. The yearly administration of state assessments of reading and math achievement, as well as growth in English proficiency, led to the realization that major changes needed to be made to the type of instruction provided by TBE/TPI resource teachers.

Since ELL students are going to be assessed on their achievement in reading and math, significant instruction time for students in these two core areas. In addition, to be effective, the instruction delivered must be comprehensible to students, regardless of their level of English proficiency. Strategies such as the use of the T-BAR for assessment and the BIIP to plan for differentiated instruction for each student were initiated (see Chapters 1 and 4 for further discussion). In this manner, assessment has indeed driven instruction.

ESL levels are defined through both formal and informal assessments and instruction in the resource classroom has focused on building literacy for ELLs. Bilingual teachers in our district have grown in their knowledge of teaching literacy through department and district staff development opportunities. And, as their students have been included in the accountability system through state testing, bilingual teachers have focused more on improving their skills as literacy educators. Based on these needs, courses were organized to give teachers more literacy tools. Book clubs, focus groups, and salary lane credit courses have been offered that teach a variety of skills for teachers to implement balanced and responsive literacy programs for ELLs. Again, because assessment has driven instruction, it has also driven the need for targeted staff development.

Conclusion

In this chapter, two teachers and a coordinator contributed their personal accounts of how they use multiple sources of assessment data to affect ELLs' learning, both at the classroom level and at the program level. At the classroom level, bilingual teachers use assessment data from the pivotal portfolio in order to:

- Discover students' strengths and weaknesses and design appropriate program of instruction

- Make decisions about student transitioning from first-language literacy to English literacy

- Inform their colleagues about ELL students' progress and make collaborative decisions on behalf of students

- Recommend students for gifted education, as well as for intervention and/or special education programs

- Determine student's readiness to exit from the TBE program while ensuring their academic success

At the program level, coordinators use the same rich data in order to:

- Review students' progress with teachers

- Coach individual teachers in making the most appropriate instructional decisions for ELL students

- Monitor program effectiveness and make improvements

- Guide staff development decisions

As this chapter has demonstrated, a coherent assessment plan that guides data collection, analysis, and use is a powerful tool for educators who work collaboratively to meet the language and learning needs of all of their students.

Questions for Reflection and Action

1. Because she has collected data about her student's learning over time and from different sources over time, Mrs. Alibhai was able to recruit the support of other teachers to provide the most appropriate instruction for him. Reflect on your own students' performances in the classroom and identify one student who may need special services. What types of data have you collected on the student? What other information would you need to have richer portrait of him/her as a learner?

2. Identify five strategies that you learned from Mrs. Williams that can be applied to your own setting to help your students transition from their first language to English literacy? What instructional changes would you make based on the assessment results you have about your current students' performances to encourage a more successful transition?

3. What kinds of events or data inform your program improvement practices? After reading Mrs. Wojtysiak's account of her role as a program coordinator, what factors would you consider when making program improvements? Why?

Developing an Evaluation Framework for Language Education Programs

Chapter Overview

This chapter addresses authentic accountability that is internal to schools, districts, or programs. We show how information from evaluation, when overlaid onto the BASIC model, can be useful in determining the effectiveness of language education programs. We then summarize a longitudinal evaluation study that illustrates the development, implementation, and evaluation of Schaumburg School District 54's dual language program.

Guiding Questions

- To what extent does your school, district, or program have internal accountability? What evidence do you have to make that claim?
- What criteria are currently considered by your school, district, or state in evaluating your language education programs?
- What types of research questions might you ask in proposing an evaluation study for your language education program?

Key Concepts

- Internal accountability (of language education programs) is powerful, as it is shaped by the people who are impacted by the results.
- Program evaluation offers opportunities for constituents to give targeted feedback and use information for improving services.
- Data from evaluation research help validate our assumptions about how language education programs function.

The BASIC model revolves around student assessments that are representative of program goals and learning standards. The data from these assessments are used to inform curriculum and instruction for teachers and administrators in language education programs. Previous chapters described formative and summative assessments designed to answer questions about students' growth over time in language proficiency and academic achievement, and their attainment of these goals. In addition, such data give teachers insight into students' increasing cross-cultural competence.

The data derived from assessment can be used not only to make decisions about students but also to judge the effectiveness of the programs themselves. Evaluation acts as a barometer, so to speak, of authentic accountability systems; it is an internal index of the functioning of educational programs. Evaluation data allow constituents to assign worth to individual components of language education programs as well as to the program as a whole.

This chapter revolves around the critical question, what are the components that of evaluation frameworks for language education programs, and how can they reflect authentic accountability? To answer this question, we begin by superimposing evaluation onto the BASIC model as a means of systematically exploring program effectiveness. By extending the model to embrace evaluation, we have a more complete picture of authentic accountability. Moreover, the data collected in language education programs can be used both for student assessment and for program evaluation—an extension of the BASIC model's usefulness.

After a general discussion of evaluation of language education programs using the BASIC model, we give a concrete example in the form of an evaluation study that Schaumburg School District 54 conducted on its dual language program in 2002. The results demonstrate the benefits of dual language education for the target population and are intended to contribute to the national conversation about effective programs for language learners.

Using the BASIC Model for Program Evaluation

The BASIC model offers an integrated perspective on examining data related to language education programs. As its name suggests, its intent is to help teachers and administrators develop balanced assessment and accountability systems that are inclusive and comprehensive. One of the purposes of authentic accountability is to highlight the value of educational services and pinpoint challenging areas in need of improvement based on evidence from evaluation. The evaluation data in an authentic accountability system are:

- Expressions of the internal functioning of schools and school districts while responsive to external accountability mandates

- Shared with teachers, administrators, and the greater community

- Comprehensive, reflective of learning standards, learning benchmarks, and learning goals

- Systemic, representative of language education programs as a whole

- Valid indicators of student performance and program effectiveness.

In Figure 7.1, program evaluation is superimposed on the BASIC model. Not only is the integrity of the model retained, but the figure shows how program evaluation proceeds within the context of the model. Each component is connected to others, so that collectively, a powerful information network is formed, representing a systematic approach to the evaluation of language education programs.

In this expanded framework, the examination of evidence from assessment and other sources determines the extent to which learning goals, learning standards, and learning benchmarks are being met. Ultimately, conclusions regarding the effectiveness of language education programs are evaluative in nature; they involve the interpretation of quantitative and qualitative data, along with professional judgment. Decision making is inherently a human process, and as educators, we strive to be as fair and impartial as possible. The BASIC model can systematize how we view evaluation and use the data generated from it to improve teaching and learning.

The efficacy of the model itself may be explored through evaluation research in other language education contexts. Because many school districts may be hesitant to use formative assessment data as part of their accountability equation, some of the first questions to answer are the following:

- To what extent do formative data help inform or explicate summative state or district data?

- What additional information is gleaned from formative data that give greater understanding of language education programs and the students served?

- Are there specific measures that better inform accountability than others, and, if so, how can we maximize their usefulness?

- How does teacher involvement in data-driven decisions affect programmatic cohesion and student performance?

- Do parent support and community impact make a difference in program functioning?

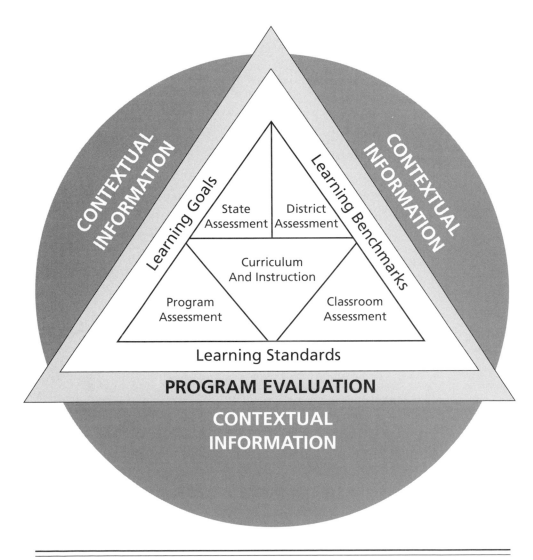

Figure 7.1 The BASIC model with program evaluation superimposed.

The example from School District 54 illustrates the efficacy of the BASIC model in practice and demonstrates how educators can collaborate in their efforts to balance internal and external accountability at the local level.

A Global Framework for Evaluation

In the BASIC model, evaluation is internal to the functioning of language education programs and is viewed as one component of program operation. This relationship does not preclude use of the model for external purposes as well, such as to show compliance with federal guidelines. In the broadest understanding, evaluation is one aspect of information gathering for use in program design, implementation, and refinement.

Evaluation should be considered one part of a cyclical and iterative process (rather than an isolated event), because it interacts with other aspects of program implementation. Program evaluation encompasses an examination of theory and research on language acquisition, acculturation, and academic achievement, and it should ground learning goals and learning standards and align them with student assessment. Formative and summative assessment measures should be examined for reliability, validity, fairness, and practicality. The data generated from these measures then help formalize program outcomes, which in turn lead to refinement of curriculum and instruction, along with improved services.

As an extension of the BASIC model, the assessment principles introduced in Chapter 2 are evident in this evaluation framework. Assessment Principle 1—Teaching and learning are influenced by the interaction among learning goals, learning standards, and learning benchmarks and their alignment with assessment measures—is clearly articulated in program implementation. Assessment Principles 2 and 3, combined under student assessment, encourage the use of formative and summative measures at the local, district, and state levels to yield rich quantitative, qualitative, or combined types of evidence. Assessment Principle 4, which distinguishes students' language proficiency from their academic achievement, is the target of program outcomes. Finally, Assessment Principle 5—Well-articulated goals that stem from a program's mission and vision, are formulated, shared, and supported by all constituents—helps guide the evaluation process.

A Framework for Generating Data for Authentic Accountability

Authentic accountability is distinct from externally imposed accountability in that it emanates internally from a program itself and is contextualized within that setting. It is the context that enables educators to connect the dots and see relationships among the program's components. Authentic accountability is more comprehensive and inclusive than accountability solely driven by external requirements because it includes locally relevant data..

For example, to fulfill the mandates of the No Child Left Behind (NCLB) Act, accountability for language education programs could be addressed by having learning standards anchored in and aligned with summative district and state assessments. However, the BASIC model brings both formative and summative assessments into the fold, and these assessments fill in the gaps left by the purely quantitative, annual data from summative assessment.

In an era with such a prominent focus on accountability, educational decision making is data driven. However, assessment data are not meaningful without a context. We recall from Chapter 2 that the BASIC model is influenced by community and student characteristics, the mission and vision of the language education program, and the interests of major constituents, including students, parents, teachers, administrators, and boards of education. As discussed in Chapter 2 and illustrated with the example of School District 54, the components of the BASIC model are readily adapted to reflect individual language education programs (e.g., dual language programs, transitional bilingual programs, English-only programs) in other settings.

Of particular importance to our discussion of authentic accountability here is the influence of the major constituents. Questions for the different audiences and stakeholders should be included in program evaluation:

- What are the attitudes of students, parents, teachers, and administrators toward the language education program?

- How do students and parents benefit from the services offered?

- How can students themselves be part of the process?

The answers to these questions frame evaluation and provide context to the program's operation; in addition, they aid in determining to what degree the program can be considered effective from the perspective of the various constituents. Observation, surveys, and interviews with teachers, administrators, parents, and students are important barometers of program functioning. When examined alongside formative and summative data from multiple measures, the data become relevant, meaningful, and useful to those directly involved. Thus, accountability, and the evaluation associated with it, no longer pose threats to administrators and teachers but are viewed as necessary and essential, and are welcomed for generating data useful for making sound educational decisions.

External accountability often rests on a narrow interpretation of student-generated data that are quantifiable. Authentic accountability views evaluation from a broader perspective that includes both quantitative and qualitative perspectives. Student data from high-stakes tests are not the sole source of input in an accountability equation; for evaluation purposes, student data from summative and formative measures, matched to specific demographic characteristics, contribute to overall programmatic information.

Student assessment data form the nucleus of accountability. The more sources of data, the better informed decisions will be. Worksheet 17 in the Appendix is a decision-making matrix based on the BASIC model. Included are the three major types of assessment, the purposes for assessment, potential decisions to be made at different levels, and specific data to be collected via formative and summative measures. The last column is the most telling; it displays teachers' or administrators' estimates of the extent to which data are used to inform decision making. The worksheet is intended as a needs assessment for those who work in language education programs to better understand the important role of data in their educational setting.

Once there is an awareness of the types of data-driven decisions to be made in language education programs, the next step is the creation of an action plan. Worksheet 18 asks questions of teachers and administrators on the use of evaluation data (identified in the first part of the worksheet) for authentic accountability purposes. Central to the discussion are the plan's goals, actions, resources, and persons responsible. With data of this sort in hand, the strengths of the accountability system currently in place and the areas that need to be strengthened can be identified for language education programs. Part of the planning also entails figuring out which professional development activities best serve language education professionals.

The BASIC model provides a conceptual scheme for envisioning evaluation as part of authentic accountability for language education programs. Using evaluation frameworks, the BASIC model is recast to accommodate programmatic data. These frameworks are designed as a starting point for a discussion of the systematic use of information by teachers and administrators to refine and improve their language education programs. Over time, assessment data can be used for program evaluation purposes. Carefully designed evaluation studies help meet both internal and external accountability requirements. Internally, the goal is to use information gleaned from program evaluation to make structural and curricular improvements that lead to improved teaching and learning. Externally, it is important for programs to meet student achievement goals set by state and federal policies, and demonstrate program effectiveness. Furthermore, evaluation data can be used to influence policy on the local, state, and national levels by providing empirical evidence about the types of language education programs most effective for ELLs and English speakers relative to the goals of English language development, academic learning, the development of languages other than English, and cross-cultural competence. We strongly believe that empirical evidence of actual student performance and development over time must inform policies about language education in this country.

Evaluating the Dual Language Program in School District 54: A Longitudinal Study

This part of the chapter illustrates how the BASIC model can be used to guide program evaluation. We summarize a report of a longitudinal study conducted on the dual language program of School District 54 between 1996 and 2002. So that language educators can replicate this study in other contexts, the steps taken to ensure a quality study are discussed, and data collection and analysis methods are described. The results of the evaluation study are presented, with attention to implications for program and professional development.

Context of the Study

This post hoc longitudinal study examines the maturational development of the dual language program (kindergarten through eighth grade) in one school of School District 54 between 1994 and 2002. MacArthur

School began the English-Spanish dual language program with assistance from a federal, Title VII grant. School District 54's dual language program follows the implementation of an 80/20 dual language model. In an 80/20 program, in kindergarten, the target language other than English is used as the medium of instruction 80% of the time and English is used 20% of the time.. The amount of English used as the language of instruction is increased by 10% each subsequent year until the instructional language allocation reaches a 50/50 ratio by fourth or fifth grade. This ratio is maintained in subsequent years. Such a design allows students the opportunity to develop full proficiency in the Spanish language within a broader social environment that is almost always English dominant.

The dual language program at MacArthur School is a program of choice that is open to all students in the school district, with admission preference given to MacArthur's neighborhood students and to the siblings of student participants. It began with one kindergarten class in the 1994–95 school year as its first cohort. Each year thereafter, a grade level was added until the 2000–01 school year. After the next two years, the initial group graduated from Eisenhower Junior High School, having completed eighth-grade.

Admission to the program requires a formal application and a parent interview with the principal; thereafter a lottery system is used to ensure equal access to admission. Admission to the program is inclusive by nature, thus accommodating special education students, typically developed youth, as well as gifted students.

During the first years of the program, considerable effort went into curriculum design and into developing an authentic assessment system that was aligned with learning goals and learning standards. Collaborative teams of teachers informally evaluated the language education program each summer as the program was being built. Curricular changes were made based on summer staff's program reviews, curriculum mapping, and a few research studies that were presented at professional conferences each year from other school districts and programs. Various assessments were piloted and selected as common or standard assessments to be included in the pivotal dual language portfolio. Since the program received monies from federal grants, summative assessments were also selected to meet evaluation requirements for the grant (the longitudinal study was initiated before NCLB, so summative assessments of students' academic achievement and of ELLs' English language proficiency had not yet been mandated at the federal level). It was decided, however, to be maximally useful to teachers in improving instruction, common formative and summative classroom assessments would constitute the major part of the portfolio. Additional informal measures were also selected and used from time to time to gauge student growth in the area of cultural learning. As a result, in 1996, the dual language pivotal portfolio described in Chapter 4 became the essential assessment tool for monitoring dual language students' progress and measuring their achievement.

In 1997, as the dual language curriculum became more clearly articulated among staff members and the program's foundation was built, questions of accountability began to arise from parents as well as the larger community. Even though parents had been satisfied with their individual children's progress, as time went on, they began to ask questions about long-range academic achievement and the bilingual proficiency of dual language students as a group. In addition, other entities, such as the district's school board, other school districts in the state, and dual language advocates elsewhere, began to ask for evidence of program effectiveness. In response to these demands, a post hoc evaluation study was conducted by the two co-authors on behalf of School District 54 between 2000 and 2003, using summative data that had been collected as part of students' portfolios since 1996.

The study was presented at the Fourth International Symposium on Bilingualism in Tuscon, Arizona, in 2003 and the complete report (Gottlieb & Nguyen, 2004) was published in the symposium's proceedings.

Purpose of the Study and Research Questions

The sample in this study consisted of 265 students, 129 who used English as their native language (NES) and 134 who used Spanish as their native language (NSS); two students came from other language backgrounds. Overall, 16% of the group was eligible for free and reduced lunch. In 1996, when summative data started to be collected on students in the language education program, participating students represented three cohorts—one kindergarten class, one first-grade class, and one second-grade class. By 2002, the year the study was analyzed, the first cohort of students was in grade 8, and a total of 265 students were enrolled in the program. Student performance on summative tests from 1996 to 2002 were analyzed and reported in grades 2 to 6.

The purpose of the study was to investigate the growth in second language proficiency and academic achievement of two groups of students participating in the dual language program, NES and NSS, in comparison with (1) their counterparts, (2) native Spanish speakers in the transitional bilingual education program (TBE), and (3) NES in the general education program. Using multiple sources of data, the study sought to answer the following questions:

1. *Second language (L2) proficiency:* What has been the growth in the students' (NES and NSS) oral and literacy development in their second language development over time?

2. *Academic achievement in the native (L1) language:* How do NSS and NES students in the dual language program perform in their native language in language arts, reading, and mathematics, compared with their peers in the TBE program and the general education classrooms?

3. *Academic achievement in the second language for ELLs in the dual language program:* How do NSS students perform in English (L2) in language arts, reading, and mathematics, compared to their peers in the TBE classes?

Collection of Data from Multiple Sources of Summative Assessment

At the time of the study, all school districts in the state of Illinois were required to administer the *Illinois Measure of Annual Growth in English* (IMAGE) for ELLs and the Illinois Standards Achievement Test (ISAT) for English-proficient students, starting in grade 3. Although the test results were disaggregated, analyzed, and reported to the local board of education every year to answer their concerns about the performance of ELLs and other dual language students, a decision was made not to use data from the IMAGE and ISAT in this study owing to concerns about possible inconsistencies caused by changes in the test made at the state level. (This decision also illustrates the importance of having multiple sources of data to answer different accountability demands.) Instead, two norm-referenced national measures provided the data needed to answer the critical questions of the study.

The IDEA Proficiency Test (IPT), a norm-referenced language proficiency measure in the areas of listening, speaking, reading and writing was administered annually in the students' second language, Spanish for native English speakers and English for ELLs.

Between 1996 and 2003, the TerraNova test (1997), a norm-referenced measure of academic achievement in English, served as the internal accountability measure in English academic achievement in School District 54, and was administered biennially, starting in grade 2, to all proficient English-speaking students. The SUPERA test (1997), a norm-referenced measure of academic achievement in Spanish, the analogue of the English test, was administered biennially, starting in grade 2, to native Spanish-speaking ELLs in the TBE and dual language programs.

Methods of Analysis

For this study, School District 54 hired an outside evaluation firm, OER Associates, to conduct statistical analysis of students' performance on the three assessments. Tests results were collected from the district-wide assessment information system (the TerraNova) as well as from students' test results kept in their portfolios (the IPT and the SUPERA).

For the IPT measure, all available oral language, reading, and writing data from students' portfolios were combined across years 1996 to 2002. Overall language proficiency designations rather than raw scores were used from 1 (the lowest) to 3 (the highest) for reading and writing and from 1 (the lowest) to 6 (the highest) for oral proficiency. Paired t test comparisons from year to year were calculated for both groups of students in the dual language program (NES and NSS) to determine growth in their respective second language proficiency.

For the SUPERA, scores were reported in the form of normal curve equivalents (NCEs) for NSS students for each of the subscales and the total battery.

For the TerraNova, standard subscale scores in reading, language, and mathematics as well as total scores were reported for NES and non-ELL NSS students. All available TerraNova scores were combined for years 1996 to 2002 prior to analysis. Analyses of variance were conducted that compared differences among the student groups. NES students in general education classes were compared with those in the dual language program, and NSS students who were ELLs in the dual language program were compared with their ELL peers in the TBE program.

Results of the Study

Second Language Proficiency Growth: Oral Proficiency

NES students made continuous progress in acquiring Spanish oral language proficiency. From kindergarten to grade 2, students gained more than one half-level. From grades 2 to 4, the pace declined to about a third of a level per year, with a jump to a full level in grades 4 and 5. Unlike in earlier previous years, when students made statistically significant gains in oral language, in grade 6, NES speakers seem to reached the test's ceiling, and may be considered orally proficient in Spanish according to the IPT measure.

This statistic is quite revealing, as the test is normed on a native Spanish-speaking population, yet these second language learners systematically moved through the stages of second language acquisition, from non-Spanish speakers to fluent Spanish speakers, within a period of six years of participation in the dual language program.

Like their NES counterparts acquiring Spanish, NSS students who were ELLs made continuous progress in acquiring English proficiency across the grade levels. From kindergarten through grade 4, the students made statistically significant gains in oral language each year. They top out in grade 5, when they reach the test's ceiling and are considered fluent in English. NSS students reach oral language proficiency in English approximately one year earlier than NES students reach comparable proficiency in Spanish, as most of these students are exposed to spoken English prior to the onset of the program and they were in an almost exclusively English environment in the larger community. Tables 7.1 and 7.2 provide a grade-to-grade comparison for the Oral IPT proficiency levels for NES and NSS counterparts.

Second language Growth: Reading and Writing Proficiency

NES students made continuous progress in acquiring Spanish reading across the grade levels, with approximately one half-designation growth per year on the IPT. From grades 2 to 6, each year the students made statistically significant gains in Spanish reading, with a slight dip from grade 4 to grade 5.

Table 7.1 Grade-to-Grade Comparisons for Native English Speakers in Dual Language Education: Oral IPT Designation Scores

Grade Comparisons	Mean Previous Grade	Mean Current Grade	Mean Difference	Standard Difference	df	t	P
Grade K to 1	1.63	2.25	0.63	0.67	48	6.44	.001
Grade 1 to 2	2.24	2.87	0.63	0.71	38	5.46	.001
Grade 2 to 3	2.84	3.20	0.36	0.64	25	2.82	.009
Grade 3 to 4	3.21	3.53	0.32	0.58	19	−2.36	.030
Grade 4 to 5	3.55	4.55	1.00	1.11	22	4.21	.001
Grade 5 to 6	4.71	4.59	−0.12	0.60	17	−0.81	NS

NSS students made statistically significant gains in acquiring English reading from grades 2 to 3, and then tended to grow at a slower rate. It appears that this group of students reaches a plateau in English reading by grade 5, which may be an artifact of the language proficiency measure used. These trends are illustrated in Tables 7.3 and 7.4, which show grade-to-grade comparisons for NES students and their NSS counterparts.

The only educationally significant gain in writing performance in Spanish for NES students came near the start of the program. Otherwise, writing proficiency in Spanish remained rather minimal across the grade levels. This absence of substantial growth in Spanish writing points to the fact that the domain of writing was not emphasized in the curriculum at that time.

Table 7.2 Grade-to-Grade Comparisons for Native Spanish Speakers in Dual Language Education: Oral IPT Designation Scores

Grade Comparisons	Mean Previous Grade	Mean Current Grade	Mean Difference	Standard Difference	df	t	P
Grade K to 1	2.41	3.46	1.05	0.85	36	7.56	.001
Grade 1 to 2	3.26	4.50	1.24	0.85	42	9.44	.001
Grade 2 to 3	4.39	5.00	0.61	1.02	40	3.82	.001
Grade 3 to 4	4.96	5.65	0.69	0.84	26	4.21	.001
Grade 4 to 5	5.87	5.94	0.06	0.25	15	1.00	NS

Table 7.3 Grade-to-Grade Comparisons for Native English Speakers in Dual Language Education: Reading IPT Designation Scores

Grade Comparisons	Mean Previous Grade	Mean Current Grade	Mean Difference	Standard Difference	df	t	P
Grade 2 to 3	1.09	1.50	0.41	0.50	31	4.61	.001
Grade 3 to 4	1.42	2.05	0.63	0.60	19	4.61	.001
Grade 4 to 5	1.95	2.23	0.27	0.63	21	2.03	.056
Grade 5 to 6	2.13	2.69	0.56	0.51	15	4.39	.001

NSS students appear to perform at a rate commensurate with that of their NES in acquiring writing proficiency in the second language. These data substantiate the findings that both groups of students developed their second language oral proficiency at a faster rate than their second language proficiency in reading and writing. We return to this point in our discussion of implications of the study for program and professional development later in the chapter. Tables 7.5 and 7.6 are grade-to-grade comparisons of writing proficiency growth for NES and their NSS counterparts.

Academic Achievement in First and Second Languages

Overall, NSS students in the dual language program and the TBE program scored between the 47th and the 64th referenced normed curve equivalent (NCE) on the SUPERA test across grade levels 2, 4, and 6. In

Table 7.4 Grade-to-Grade Comparisons for Native Spanish Speakers in Dual Language Education: Reading IPT Designation Scores

Grade Comparisons	Mean Previous Grade	Mean Current Grade	Mean Difference	Standard Difference	df	t	P
Grade 2 to 3	1.57	2.41	0.85	0.76	45	7.57	.001
Grade 3 to 4	2.17	2.04	0.13	0.55	22	1.14	NS
Grade 4 to 5	2.08	2.33	0.25	0.45	11	1.91	.082
Grade 5 to 6	2.36	2.36	0.00	0.63	11	0.00	NS

Table 7.5 Grade-to-Grade Comparisons for Native English Speakers in Dual Language Education: Writing IPT Designation Scores

Grade Comparisons	Mean Previous Grade	Mean Current Grade	Mean Difference	Standard Difference	df	t	P
Grade 2 to 3	2.05	2.21	0.16	0.37	19	1.84	.083
Grade 3 to 4	2.29	2.00	−0.29	0.49	6	−1.55	NS
Grade 4 to 5	2.00	2.08	0.08	0.28	13	1.00	NS
Grade 5 to 6	2.00	1.87	−0.13	0.35	7	−1.00	NS

grades 2 and 4, these students hovered around the 50th NCE or 50th percentile in reading, language, and mathematics. By grade 6, NSS students in the dual language program approximated the 60th NCE for all content areas, a sizable gain (Table 7.7).

NSS students in the TBE program in School District 54 receive native language support in content areas, which gradually diminishes as students become more proficient in English. As shown in Table 7.8, by grade 4 they are scoring at the 40th to 47th NCE. In contrast, their NSS counterparts in the dual language program receive sustained Spanish instruction for at least 50% of the instructional time. At grade 4, NSS students in the dual language program consistently performed between the 59th and the 61st norm-referenced NCE in Spanish reading, language, and mathematics, thus consistently outperforming their peers in the TBE program, with statistically significant differences in reading, language, math, and the total score, irrespective of the norming group. The

Table 7.6 Grade-to-Grade Comparisons for Native Spanish Speakers in Dual Language Education: Writing IPT Designation Scores

Grade Comparisons	Mean Previous Grade	Mean Current Grade	Mean Difference	Standard Difference	df	t	P
Grade 2 to 3	1.96	2.19	0.23	0.43	25	2.74	.011
Grade 3 to 4	2.20	2.10	−0.10	0.57	9	−0.56	NS
Grade 4 to 5	2.20	2.00	−0.20	0.42	9	−1.50	NS
Grade 5 to 6	2.00	2.60	0.60	0.55	4	2.45	.070

Table 7.7 The Academic Achievement of Native Spanish Speakers in Grades 2, 4, and 6, Based on SUPERA Reading, Language, Mathematics, and Total Scores

Score	Grade 2 (N = 60)			Grade 4 (N = 72)			Grade 6 (N = 21)		
	Mean	S.D.	N	Mean	S.D.	N	Mean	S.D.	N
Reading NCE*	38.00	10.31	60	38.89	18.22	70	42.48	14.81	21
Language NCE	38.30	10.29	60	35.09	14.77	70	42.76	16.79	21
Math NCE	39.83	22.06	60	33.49	15.56	72	43.62	21.44	21
Total NCE	37.82	14.72	60	34.71	15.92	70	42.14	17.21	21
Reading Ref. NCE	47.90	16.49	60	50.71	23.00	70	60.05	18.69	21
Language Ref. NCE	46.75	14.78	60	47.60	19.18	70	58.57	16.52	21
Math Ref. NCE	52.67	20.66	60	52.33	20.58	72	64.14	22.68	21
Total Ref. NCE	50.70	19.77	60	49.43	22.35	70	61.43	17.54	21

*NCE = normal curve equivalent.

Table 7.8 A Comparison of the Academic Achievement of Grade 4 Native Spanish Speakers in Transitional Bilingual Education and Dual Language Education in Spanish (L1), Based on SUPERA Scores

Score	Transitional Bilingual Education (N = 46)		Dual Language Education (N = 26)		Mean Difference	t	P
	Mean	S.D.	Mean	S.D.			
Reading NCE	34.34	16.51	46.58	18.69	12.24	2.85	.006
Language NCE	29.93	14.18	43.81	11.42	13.88	4.24	.001
Math NCE	29.74	13.80	40.11	16.54	10.38	2.85	.006
Total NCE	29.50	14.15	43.54	15.05	14.04	3.92	.001
Reading Ref. NCE	45.21	22.18	60.04	21.69	14.83	2.73	.008
Language Ref. NCE	40.84	18.28	59.04	14.96	18.20	4.29	.001
Math Ref. NCE	47.48	18.57	60.92	21.50	13.45	2.79	.007
Total Ref. NCE	42.29	20.04	61.50	21.15	19.21	3.80	.001

differences in the performance of these two groups of students attest to the impact of native language instruction on ELL students' academic performance.

Based on the results of the TerraNova tests, NES students in the dual language program outperformed their peers in the general education classes in reading, language, mathematics, and the total score, more significantly in grade 2 than in grades 4 or 6. It can be inferred from these results that initial native language literacy for the NES students in the dual language program has been strong despite use of the 80/20 model. It affirms the curricular choice made at the onset of the program to build native language literacy first for all students.

By grade 6, academic achievement in English is comparable for both groups of NES students. However, for the NES students in the dual language program, academic achievement in English is only half of the academic learning equation (Table 7.9). These results show that math and literacy achievement in English for NES students in the dual language program remains on the same course as their counterparts' achievement in the general education program while they gain the additional benefit of second language proficiency.

The TerraNova results were also used to compare academic achievement of NSS in English with the achievements of their ELL counterparts

Table 7.9 Matrix of Pairwise Differences and Comparison Probabilities of the Academic Achievement of Native English Speakers in General Education and Dual Language across Grade Levels, Based on TerraNova Scores

	Grade 2 General Education		Grade 4 General Education		Grade 6 General Education	
Status	Mean Diff.	P	Mean Diff.	P	Mean Diff.	P
Reading						
Dual Lang. NES	14.964	.101	18.376	.065	0.767	NS
Language						
Dual Lang. NES	11.089	NS	10.062	NS	6.749	NS
Math						
Dual Lang. NES	17.356	.061	2.413	NS	6.911	NS
Total Score						
Dual Lang. NES	14.483	.063	9.699	NS	0.141	NS

in the TBE program. The results show no significant differences in math scores between these two groups at any grade level. However, in grades 2 and 4, there were statistically significant differences in reading and overall achievement, with students in the dual language program consistently outperforming their counterparts in the TBE program (Table 7.10). These results show the impact of long-term, robust native language instruction on academic achievement in a second language.

Overall Findings and Interpretation

Dual language education, with its short history in the United States, is still being questioned as to its contribution to the educational repertoire for students in comparison with other language programs. It is uniquely complex in that specific decisions are made that may differentially impact two distinct groups of second language learners that make up the sample. Our study affirms the language goals of the dual language program by showing that NES and NSS students, though culturally and linguistically different, benefit from dual language educational experiences. The language development and academic achievement of the two groups seem to follow a similar path.

Table 7.10 Matrix of Pairwise Differences and Comparison Probabilities between Native Spanish Speakers in Transitional Bilingual Education and Dual Language Programs on Academic Achievement in English (L2) across Grade Levels, Based on TerraNova Scores

Status	Transitional Bilingual Education Grade 2		Transitional Bilingual Education Grade 4		Transitional Bilingual Language Grade 6	
	Mean Diff.	*P*	*Mean Diff.*	*P*	*Mean Diff.*	*P*
Reading						
Dual Lang. NSS	63.417	.001	29.883	.007	2.037	NS
Language						
Dual Lang. NSS	27.537	NS	21.106	.086	−13.792	NS
Math						
Dual Lang. NSS	30.667	NS	17.875	NS	1.565	NS
Total Score						
Dual Lang. NSS	39.389	.027	22.901	.017	−3.301	NS

Overall, second language oral proficiency is strong, and remains strong, for both groups of language learners. It appears that both groups of students have a solid foundation in the development of listening and speaking skills in their second language. In contrast, literacy development in the second language for both of these groups, in particular writing, was not as robust.

After six years of dual language education, the academic achievement of NES students in the dual language program is comparable with that of their counterparts in the general education program. In addition, they have acquired both language proficiency and conceptual understanding in Spanish, their second language. This finding underscores the effectiveness of the dual language program as a language education as well as an academic instructional program.

After six years of dual language education, NSS students' performance is comparable to that of their counterparts in the TBE program. In addition, their academic performance in Spanish in the later years remains stronger. This finding points to the importance of native language support for ELLs in academic subjects as they acquire their second language, irrespective of the instructional model. Moreover, the results indicate the potential of the dual language model as a vehicle for not only transitioning students into English but at the same time strengthening ELL students' native language skills and thus enriching students' potential for academic success. These findings are consistent with empirical research in the field that demonstrate the effectiveness of dual language programs for English speakers and for English language learners (Collier & Thomas, 2004; Genesee, et. al., 2006; Lindholm-Leary, 2001).

For a second language program to be both effective and equitable, it must equally address and differentiate the needs of subgroups of second language learners participating in the program. Through a rigorous evaluation study, educators in School District 54 are able to provide evidence that indeed, dual language education presents a valid alternative approach in language education to provide a diverse group of students with differentiated language and academic instruction that leads to bilingualism and academic success for all students.

At the local level, the evaluation study we conducted yielded achievement information that supports student's growth observed in the classroom through formative assessment. It also clarified areas of improvement that need to be addressed, namely, students' acquisition skills in writing.

Using Results from the Evaluation Study to Improve the Language Education Program

The study results indicate that an area of weakness in students' achievement was their writing skills, especially in Spanish. This finding was reported to dual language teachers and administrators at a meeting at the beginning of the year in 2004. At subsequent meetings, teachers discussed plans for strengthening students' writing skills. Teachers participated in professional development classes on implementing a writing workshop in their classrooms. They collaborated in designing classroom activities to build writing skills for students in both languages. Evidence of their focus on writing was presented in Chapter 5, in Ms. Hernandez's account of her writing instruction. Although many writing assessment tools exist with which to evaluate students' development in English (for both NES and NSS students) and to set goals, teachers found that Spanish development is an area that lacks clarity and specificity as far as expectations are concerned. Eventually, to address this need, the Spanish as a Second Language (SSL) checklist was created that includes expected skill development in oral, reading, and writing skills at each grade (see Worksheet 13 in the Appendix). This instrument helps teachers set expectation for oral proficiency, reading, and writing development in Spanish for all NES students.

The combination of support for teachers in improving writing instruction through the use of the writing workshop, along with efforts to clarify Spanish as a second language targets to parallel the existing English as a second language targets, help to address the area of weakness found in the program evaluation study. Program improvements were made as a direct response to this study's results. In this manner, evaluation studies serve not only as a response to external demands of accountability, but also are instrumental in targeting areas of program improvement as a part of internal accountability practices.

Conclusion

The first part of this chapter illustrated how evaluation frameworks can be superimposed on the BASIC model. The second part of the chapter reported on a longitudinal evaluation study conducted in School District 54's dual language program that investigated and documented program effectiveness for ELLs and English speakers. The study also compared results of ELLs in the dual language program with their counterparts in the TBE program, and English speakers to their counterparts in the English-only general education program in School District 54. This longitudinal study contributes to the research base that supports dual language education for all students. Language educators in other contexts are encouraged to use the BASIC model to evaluate their language education programs, and to use empirical evidence on their students' growth and achievement to make informed decisions about their policies, programs, and practices for language learners.

Questions for Reflection and Action

1. Re-examine the components of the BASIC model. How might they apply in the design of a plan for authentic accountability at your school or school district?

2. Consider the constituents served by your language education program. What questions might you pose to them to evaluate the impact of language services?

3. Think about the data currently available to you as a teacher or administrator. How might you conduct your own action research to ascertain answers about the services you provide?

Making It Work in Your Language Education Program: Lessons from the Field

Chapter Overview

In this concluding chapter, we review the critical elements of the BASIC model and share lessons learned from the implementation of this assessment and accountability system in Schaumburg School District 54. The BASIC model is used in this book to build a case and make a plea to educators to systemically use relevant and purposeful assessment practices in language education programs across the nation in order to better effect teaching and learning for all students.

Guiding Questions

- What characteristics of the BASIC model make it a viable assessment and accountability system worthy of consideration? What makes it both theoretically sound and applicable to language education programs in schools and school districts today?
- What are the phases of implementation recommended for implementing the BASIC model in a language education program? What practices should inform each phase?
- What staff development activities are necessary to ensure institutionalized implementation of the BASIC Model?

Key Concepts

- The implementation of the BASIC Model in a local school system requires a well articulated plan that is implemented in several phases.
- The involvement and leadership of teachers are critical in building an assessment system that is robust in its content yet flexible in its structure to allow teachers to use it to best meet the need of students in their classrooms.
- Any viable assessment system must first and foremost improve teaching and learning at the classroom level.

Throughout this book, we have presented a case for using an authentic assessment and accountability system in language education programs using the BASIC model. The BASIC model includes formative and summative assessments that are tied to curriculum and instruction, guided by learning goals and learning standards, grounded in contextual information, and responsive to all major constituents, including decision makers at the classroom, program, district, and state level, as well as family and community members.

Five essential assessment principles were detailed for language education programs:

1. Teaching and learning are influenced by the interaction among learning goals, learning standards, and learning benchmarks, with assessment measures.

2. Decision making is based on multiple measures that include information from formative and summative assessment across levels of implementation to yield a rich array of quantitative, qualitative, and combined types of evidence.

3. Assessment at the state and district levels is offset by assessment measures that are strongly supported at the program and classroom levels.

4. Students' language proficiency, as demonstrated by their growth in language development, is distinct from their academic achievement, their attainment of conceptual skills and knowledge. The assessment of language proficiency and academic achievement is unique, with each measure specifically crafted to fulfill a specific purpose.

5. Well-articulated learning goals that stem from a program's vision and mission are formulated, shared, and supported by all constituents, including students, parents, teachers, administrators, and boards of education.

Students' cross-cultural attitudes and behaviors are also informally observed and surveyed in language education programs.

Throughout this book, we have also given examples of ways educators can select and implement common assessments and organize them using the pivotal portfolio. The information that educators systematically collect and analyze across classes in the program and across programs in the district can be used internally to improve teaching, learning, program, and professional development. This information can also be used externally to meet state and district accountability demands. In this way, the pivotal portfolio becomes a powerful tool for communicating across levels of program implementation and with all major constituents.

The BASIC model is more than a theoretically and pedagogically sound assessment and accountability model for language education programs; it emerged from and is grounded in practice. We have included testimonies and authentic examples of assessment data to illustrate how teachers, students, and administrators use evidence to guide their decision making at classroom, program, and district levels and to respond to public accountability questions about program effectiveness.

In the course of exploring the BASIC model, we have included examples of locally developed instruments that can be replicated by other school districts. We have also provided worksheets and checklists to guide educators as they seek to improve their current assessment practices and build an authentic assessment and accountability system using the BASIC model as a framework. In this chapter we provide practical advice and strategies for educators who are interested in constructing a balanced assessment system using the BASIC model for language education programs in their local schools and school districts.

Constructing the Framework

As was detailed in Chapter 3, the construction of a local assessment system framework that is appropriate for a particular language education program using the BASIC model follows four distinct phases:

1. Establishing a global framework for assessment

2. Determining the specifics of the plan

3. Implementing the plan

4. Reviewing and revising the plan.

These four phases must be cyclical in order to keep the assessment system current with new standards and requirements while being relevant to the education of language students in the local community.

The Design Team

The major roles in building and implementing a viable assessment system are assumed by the program director and the assessment specialist in a school district. When a specialist is not available internally, it is important to seek advice and guidance from an external expert. This is analogous to working with an architect when trying to build a home. The expert knowledge about best practices in assessment that the specialist brings to the task complements the experience of the director as a language educator and administrator.

At the local level, envisioning and building an assessment system is best done collaboratively by teachers and administrators. The combined knowledge and perspectives that are brought to bear on the task help the team build an assessment system that is responsive to local needs. A team made of individuals from diverse professional backgrounds can identify the needs of all students and thus help find solutions that build an inclusive assessment system.

Phase 1: Establishing a Global Framework for Assessment

An authentic assessment and accountability framework for language learners must:

- Be guided by learning standards, learning goals, and learning benchmarks for language learning and academic achievement.

- Utilize multiple types of assessment for multiple purposes collected over multiple points in time for decision making.

- Balance summative and formative purposes of assessment with different types of assessment data.

- Serve the purpose of informing teaching and learning decisions.

- Use data to comply with accountability demands and improve program services.

- Be robust in its content yet flexible enough in its structure to accommodate changes.

- Be responsive to local school and community practices and relevant to local educational concerns.

State and district assessments are externally imposed. They are designed for state and district accountability purposes and are based on a narrow notion of accountability that relies exclusively on standardized test data for summative purposes. Formative assessment, on the other hand, is internally driven, with the appropriate kinds of assessments determined by consensus, with input from language teachers and administrators. Formative assessments are designed to monitor student progress periodically and can be used to make instructional and program improvements.

Balancing the selection of different types of assessment—standardized, standard, and idiosyncratic—helps schools maximize the value of each type of data collected as well as the collective use of all data to yield rich information that can serve multiple purposes. It is the triangulation of the three types of assessment that renders the BASIC model robust in its capacity to give authentic student information. As information gained from one type of assessment interacts with information from another type, detailed portraits of students' learning emerge. This rich pool of information about learning can then be used to inform teaching and learning at all levels of the educational system.

Phase 2: Determining the Specifics of the Plan

Once the design team has established the global assessment framework, it is in a position to review current assessment practices and identify assessment strengths and needs. When reviewing current assessment practices, it is important that the review be as comprehensive as possible and include different kinds of assessments. The review must be conducted for each major area of learning, with program goals used as a guide.

An efficient system avoids duplicating assessment measures while still providing enough information for educators to answer the major questions about student learning and program effectiveness. The pivotal portfolio, the central pillar of the assessment system, should be slim to avoid overwhelming teachers and students with redundant and irrelevant assessment. As part of the review of the system, each major assessment tool that is currently used is also be evaluated for its applicability and relevance to student learning in the language education program.

The next step is to identify and select a set of common assessments that help meet assessment goals in each of the identified learning areas. This task requires achieving a balance between, on the one hand, providing relevant, useful assessments to students and teachers for the purpose of classroom learning and teaching, and on the other hand, meeting the external accountability requirements of the school district or the state. In making decisions about assessment measures, it is advantageous to select assessments that can be used for more than one purpose and to be conservative in the selection. In the case of mandated state testing, although it is important to collect summative data on student achievement, in a comprehensive and balanced assessment system such data are complemented by other formative assessments. These assessments help to confirm or complement achievement test results, thus providing a more comprehensive view of student learning by measuring growth as well as achievement.

In developing the local assessment framework, educators will run up against the tension of assessment versus instruction. The reduced time available for teaching since the No Child Left Behind (NCLB) Act came into effect has been a major concern for classroom teachers. It is imperative that, as we construct assessment systems, we give high priority to instruction. This underscores the importance of including teachers in the construction of the assessment system: teachers help safeguard and protect the instructional priorities for students.

Even though assessment guides instruction, assessment practices must not overwhelm and direct instruction to the extent that there is no room left for individual teachers to exercise their professional discretion and judgment. Balancing minimal summative assessment requirements with ample classroom-based, formative assessment has proved to be an effective strategy for building a comprehensive system that is responsive to students' learning while giving teachers flexibility in implementation. To avoid loading the classroom with assessment requirements that interfere with instructional time, each common assessment must be carefully selected to complement other assessments in the system. In this way, a variety of information can be obtained from multiple sources that will be useful to students in improving their own learning, to teachers in improving their teaching, and to administrators in improving programs of instruction. Secondarily, data are collected to show achievement by groups of students in core areas of learning and to answer external accountability requirements. In the end, time spent on assessment must not exceed or interfere with time spent on teaching and learning.

In design and organization, then, the pivotal portfolio must be constructed with the student and classroom teacher in mind as the primary users of the information. The more an assessment can be integrated with teaching and learning, the more valuable it becomes to the assessment system. Formative assessments that are classroom-based and quantifiable, such as rubrics, can fulfill the dual purpose of being motivational tools for students and classroom accountability measures for teachers. Rubrics that are well designed provide scoring guides for powerful performance based assessments (Arter, 2006b).

Once the specific formative and summative assessments have been selected, it is helpful to chart an assessment timeline that includes all common assessments. Once the timeline is completed, it needs to be tested in real time with real school calendars. Changes to the timeline are then made to reflect the feasibility of administering assessments in real time.

Phase 3: Implementing the Plan

Since a comprehensive assessment framework includes multiple assessments, it can be challenging for teachers to learn to use many new assessments at once. It is advisable to prioritize assessments and to introduce only a few new changes at a time. The system can also be overwhelming for new teachers and for experienced teachers who are not used to multiple assessments. Staff development, therefore, is at the heart of the implementation phase of any effective assessment system. Teachers need focused and sustained professional development to ensure that they clearly understand the purpose of the assessments they use, and to ensure that they know how to use these assessments effectively within their classrooms and consistently across classrooms throughout the language education program. This, of course, requires time and collaboration.

Any complex system needs an organizing device. The BASIC model requires multiple assessments in multiple areas of learning that can interact with each other to serve multiple purposes related to the improvement of teaching and learning as well as accountability. Excellent organization keeps teachers from being overwhelmed and losing sight of the primary purpose of assessment. The pivotal portfolio helps teachers and students alike navigate the complex system of assessment, and helps organize data in ways that make the information understandable and useful.

Since the pivotal portfolio is an organizing device for teachers to make sense of and use assessment data, the information in the portfolio should be up to date at all times. The portfolio is the central tool for training teachers to use evidence to make instructional decisions. Staff development and coaching need to be provided on a regular basis to guide teachers in using the assessment information in the portfolio as the basis for discussing their students' learning progress and needs. Although designing and instating an assessment system using the BASIC model can be exciting, the success of the venture is measured not by its design but rather in the institutionalization of solid assessment practices in the system.

One of the main purposes of having a pivotal portfolio that is representative of a balanced, comprehensive system of assessment is to help educators make instructional decisions based on authentic evidence of student learning. This practice of evidence-based decision making is quite difficult to institutionalize, as many teachers would rather speculate about their student's learning than use assessments' results. Therein lies the main challenge of implementation.

The successful implementation of a comprehensive assessment system entails staff development that is anchored in collaboration. Although there are many roads to collaboration, the axioms shared here are lessons gained from Schaumburg School District 54.

Axiom 1: First, build a healthy professional learning community.

Since its reorganization in 1995, the bilingual department of School District 54 has followed a team-based model for decision making. In Chapter 1, the design of these teams was described. Teachers belong to various teams that intersect and serve different purposes. Through collaborative decision making, teachers in the program rotate into and out of leadership roles often, depending on the task at hand. Before any practice is institutionalized, it is communicated, piloted, and discussed in a variety of team settings. Staff development plans and implementation result from discussions held in teams at various levels of leaderships. Over time, a community of bilingual professional teachers has been created. These teachers share a common vision for language education in our local schools. Most important in creating this community is the high degree of professionalism that is expected of, and respected in, every teacher. Mutual accountability and mutual benefit are built in to every task to keep teachers collaborating with one another.

The concept of collaboration within professional learning communities, (PLC), though not entirely new, has recently regained attention in the field of education through the work of Dufour, Dufour, Eaker and Karhanek (2004). The practice of collaborative decision making and mutual accountability is also at the heart of their work with schools to help teachers be accountable for all children. In the gradual implementation of the assessment system, it is imperative that classroom teachers play the major role in all stages of the process. Whenever possible, teacher leadership should be encouraged and utilized.

Axiom 2: Insist that instructional decisions at all levels be evidenced-based.

For teachers to find the assessment system useful, they must see that the assessment information helps them make sound decisions for children. Requiring and modeling the use of portfolio information to make instructional decision has proved to be the best way to guide in-service teachers in using the assessment system in School District 54. Since bilingual teachers are required to use portfolio assessments to make any programmatic or instructional decisions for their students, it becomes a priority for them to learn to use these assessments, and to use them as evidence of student learning. Teachers are also asked to show evidence from multiple sources. Consequently, they are trained by practice to make instructional decisions based on more than one source of data. Since these practices are built into program procedures and standards, they provide a climate of mutual accountability among teachers for assessing students appropriately and using multiple data to inform their instruction. It takes a teacher three to five years to internalize this habit. Consequently, new teachers need frequent access to a peer coach who can help them along the way.

Axiom 3: Assist all teachers to become competent users of the assessment system.

Implementing a robust assessment system requires a robust staff development plan. Staff development should be designed to aid specific groups of teachers and provide them with differentiated learning opportunities.

In School District 54, peer coaching and mentoring have proved to be the most effective way to guide inexperienced teachers toward becoming more competent users of the assessment system. Coupled with this strategy, we use the model training of trainers as a way to build local expertise and encourage leadership among teachers. With each new internally imposed assessment practice, we typically provide intensive training at the beginning and allow teachers a reasonable amount of time to experiment with the new practice before imposing a uniform mandate for practice. Monthly staff development meetings are devoted to small team discussions so that teachers can peer coach and address their implementation concerns with one another. Teachers typically have two to three years to learn and implement a new assessment practice.

For experienced teachers who want to improve their skills beyond the minimal requirements, book clubs or focus groups with built-in incentives are offered. Surveys are used to gauge the extent to which a new assessment practice has been mastered by teachers and to identify the need for additional staff development. Also, teacher input is sought on a regular basis in team meetings to identify needed support for all teachers to reach minimal competency in implementing a new common assessment.

Staff development can only be effective when it is coupled with consistent and effective implementation. Frequent changes are not recommended. Peer coaching can be used for teachers to help each other in the implementation of each assessment.

One of the most critical parts of the effective implementation of assessment is the effective communication of the purpose and result of the assessment to students and parents. Teachers need to be informed not only on how to use assessment as an information gathering and evaluation device but also on ways to use this information to give their students helpful feedback and encourage learning. The powerful use of assessment for learning ultimately involves the student in every phase of the implementation and results in students being motivated enough to take control of their own learning (Stiggins, 2006b).

The role of the principal as an instructional leader in the successful implementation of the BASIC model cannot be emphasized enough. In schools where principals are well-informed and involved in the process, more positive instructional changes can be made through their leadership. In some cases, principals' interests and instructional priorities may not be fully aligned with those of the program, and these differences need to be resolved before any comprehensive assessment plan can be fully implemented.

Axiom 4: Persist in the quest for a quality and equitable system of assessment and evaluation for all learners.

As the pendulum of assessment swings through time, the most important lesson learned has been the need for quality. Every day brings new ideas about what constitutes best practice in education, and it is tempting to try to make changes for change's sake. As each school seeks to improve teaching and learning on a regular basis, changes will be made to the assessment system to accommodate new instructional and program demands. These changes should, however, be made in accordance with the principles of good assessment practice.

In the end, all students deserve to know how well they are doing in school and what steps are necessary for them to progress in their learning journey. A balanced assessment and accountability system such as the one described in this book ensures that educators have enough information to help each student take that next critical step in her learning.

Phase 4: Reviewing and Revising the Plan

As each assessment is implemented, teachers can provide feedback on the feasibility and utility of each measure for the improvement of teaching and learning (its value) and the time and effort that it takes to implement the assessment (its cost). If the cost of an assessment exceeds its value, it is advisable to find an alternative means of collecting the same data. As such, the assessment framework and its implementation timeline are living documents that are constantly being adapted to meet the needs of students in the program.

A feasibility study should be conducted every three to five years to include all current assessments as well as assessments being considered for the future. To complete the feasibility study, each assessment should be reviewed according to the same criteria described in chapter 4 and Worksheet 11.

To institutionalize a new assessment practice, the following process is recommended:

- Review the assessment with an assessment goal in mind, comparing the measure or practice with other comparable assessments.

- Select and invite a small group of teachers to pilot the assessment.

- Evaluate the utility and relevance of the assessment to the primary users (students and teachers) based on teachers' feedback as a result of the pilot program.

- Provide staff development for wider implementation if the use of the instrument is supported by teachers.

- Provide time and support for teachers to learn to use the assessment correctly.

- Collect data and help teachers learn to use these data for instruction. Seek teachers' feedback before making the final decision to use this assessment as a common assessment.

- Review the value of the assessment periodically and make necessary changes.

- Replace the assessment when a better tool is found, or when the assessment no longer meet the needs of the students or the program.

Usually it takes three to five years to institutionalize the effective use of a common assessment tool. For this reason, it is important that each assessment measure be evaluated carefully before it is adopted.

Conclusion

On the eve of the reauthorization of the Elementary and Secondary Education Act, the increasing visibility of ELLs and language education is expected to have a significant impact on the discussion of how to achieve equal educational opportunities for all students. The balanced approach to assessment presented in this book is intended to help educators build a defensible system of internal and external accountability that results in improved language services in schools for all students.

Using the BASIC model to construct an inclusive and comprehensive assessment, teachers and administrators can shift assessment practices from simply looking at standardized test data to using a variety of formative and summative measures. Expanding the range of evaluations used enriches classroom practice. With time, such a robust assessment system should add to the overall validity of language education programs and provide an impetus for other schools to develop enriched language education. It should also provide authentic data about student growth and achievement that can be used both to gauge program effectiveness and to inform instructional decisions in the classroom.

Finally, the use of a balanced evaluation model should contribute in important ways to the debate on accountability—currently externally imposed—and return it to the center of learning, the classroom. Unless assessment serves the purposes of learners and teachers, the primary users of assessment information, learning and teaching improvement will remain largely untouched by a decade of emphasis on school accountability.

Questions for Reflection and Action

1. Reflect on your own assessment system and discuss possible improvements needed to make it into a viable and robust assessment system for your students. Use suggestions and strategies described in this chapter as they apply to your situation

2. Form a design team and brainstorm an implementation / improvement plan of your own assessment system. Make sure you include teachers in critical leadership positions. Construct a timeline that has well articulated phases of development.

3. Write a critical response to the ideas presented in this book. Share your success stories, challenge impractical or unsound suggestions using evidence-based arguments, suggest ideas for improvement, and send them to the authors. In turn, we thank you in advance for your contributions to our own learning.

Appendix: Worksheets

Worksheet 1   Identifying Internal Influences on Your Language Education Program Design

Directions: This figure outlines some categories of sources of influence in crafting language education programs. Use this framework to identify the sources of internal influences on your language education program design that apply to your setting.

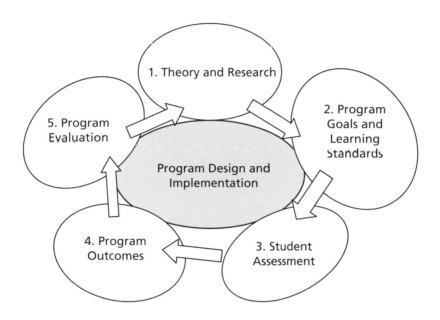

List specific sources that impact program design and implementation in your context:

1.

2.

3.

4.

5.

Worksheet 2 Considering Internal Influences on Your Program Design and Implementation

Directions: This rating scale has been created based on the five influences on program design and implementation outlined in Worksheet 1. Use the rating scale to determine to what degree these influences have been addressed in your language education program. DK = don't know; 1= strongly disagree; 2 = disagree; 3 = agree; 4 = strongly agree. Then use the information from this rating scale to identify areas to address.

Rating Scale of the Influences on Program Design in Language Education Programs	
1. Theory and research	
1.1 Review of literature yields salient issues and constructs to guide program design and implementation.	DK 1 2 3 4
1.2 Relevant scientific studies validate the program's vision, mission, and philosophy.	DK 1 2 3 4
1.3 Program data are compared to those from a body of literature.	DK 1 2 3 4
2. Program Goals and Learning Standards	
2.1 Program goals and learning standards are the guideposts for program implementation.	DK 1 2 3 4
2.2 There is alignment of program goals and learning standards with all other aspects of program design.	DK 1 2 3 4
2.2 Program goals and learning standards clearly articulate student expectations.	DK 1 2 3 4
3. Student Assessment	
3.1 Classroom, program, district, and state measures are identified.	DK 1 2 3 4
3.2. Assessment reliably and validly measures language proficiency and academic achievement in students' first and second languages.	DK 1 2 3 4
3.3 Assessment represents a balanced sampling of learning standards for both language proficiency and academic achievement.	DK 1 2 3 4
3.4 Assessment results are explained to students and parents in the language they best understand.	DK 1 2 3 4

(continued)

4. Program Outcomes	
4.1 Student outcomes are inferred from assessment data.	DK 1 2 3 4
4.2 Outcomes reflect desired growth and achievement targets.	DK 1 2 3 4
4.3 Outcomes are expressed quantitatively and qualitatively.	DK 1 2 3 4
5. Program Evaluation	
5.1 Evaluation includes timely feedback to help guide program improvement.	DK 1 2 3 4
5.2 Information from program evaluation is shared with constituents who have input in the process.	DK 1 2 3 4
5.3 Evaluation captures all aspects of program operation.	DK 1 2 3 4

Worksheet 2A   Applying Assessment Principles to Your Language Education Programs

Directions: Review current assessment practices of your language education programs. Evaluate the extent to which each assessment principle applies to your context.

Assessment Principle 1. Teaching and learning are influenced by the interaction among learning goals, learning standards and learning benchmarks with assessment measures.

Assessment Principle 2. Decision making is based on multiple measures that include information from formative and summative assessment across levels of implementation to yield a rich array of quantitative, qualitative, and combined types of evidence.

Assessment Principle 3. Assessment at the state and district levels is offset by assessment measures that are strongly supported at the program and classroom levels.

Assessment Principle 4. Students' langauge profiency, as demonstrated by their growth in language development, is distinct from their academic achievement, their attainment of conceptual skills and knowledge. The assessment of language proficiency and academic achievement is unique, with each measure specifically crafted to fulfill a specific purpose.

Assessment Principle 5. Well-articulated learning goals, which stem from a program's vision and mission, are formulated, shared, and supported by all constituents, including students, parents, teachers, administrators, and boards of education.

Worksheet 3 Identifying External Influences on Your Language Education Program and Assessment

Directions: Identify the major influences on language education in your setting. Then consider how these influences inform your language education program design and your assessment practices.

	Community and Student Characteristics	Program Mission and Goals	Major Constituents
Identify influences.			
Identify how these influences inform your language education program design.			
Identify how these influences inform your assessment practices.			

Worksheet 4 How the Components of the BASIC Model Ground and
Frame Your Language Education Program and
Assessment Practices

Directions: The first part of this worksheet presents the components that inform assessment, curriculum, and instruction in language education programs. The table includes examples of sources of contextual information that ground the BASIC model and lists the learning standards, goals, and benchmarks that frame the model. Complete the right-hand side of this table to reflect the specifics of the current reality for your language education program.

General Sources of Information for Components of the BASIC Model	Sources of Information from Your Language Education Program for Components of the BASIC model
Contextual Information (e.g., Home language surveys; Family, student & community surveys; Historical data)	**Contextual Information**
Learning Goals (e.g., Cross-cultural competence; Language development; Academic achievement)	**Learning Goals**
Learning Standards (e.g., Academic content; Language proficiency)	**Learning Standards**
Learning Benchmarks (e.g., Grade-level expectations; Growth markers along developmental continua)	**Learning Benchmarks**

Worksheet 5   Reviewing Formative Assessment
Used in Your Context

Directions: How would you describe formative assessment in your district, program, or classroom?

Step one: For each level of implementation and corresponding use of formative assessment, list the measures used in your setting on the following chart.

Step two: Compare your chart with other teachers to see
   a) if you share common assessments, and
   b) the extent to which the information from the various measures complements each other within and across the levels of implementation.

Step three: Identify strengths and weaknesses of your formative assessment system based upon this comparison.

Step four: Identify concrete ways that you can strengthen your formative assessment practices.

	Measures	**Primary Uses**
Classroom		
Program		
District		

Worksheet 6 Identifying Assessments at Each Level of Implementation in Your Context

For each level of implementation (state, district, program, classroom), identify the specific assessments used in your context to monitor students' academic learning and language development.

	State	District	Program	Classroom
Academic learning				
Language development				

Worksheet 7 Categorizing Assessments Used in Your Context by Type and Purpose

Directions: How would you categorize the assessments used in your context?

Step one: From Worksheet 6, place each assessment listed in a cell in the table below to identify its purpose(s) and type at each level of implementation as it is used in your setting. Note that an assessment may be listed more than once.

Step two: Review the table and identify the gaps in your assessment system as it is currently implemented.

Step three: Identify actions that you can take to improve your assessment system.

Level of Implementation for Assessment	Overall Purpose of Assessment	Type of Assessment		
		Idiosyncratic	Standard	Standardized
State	Formative			
	Summative			
District	Formative			
	Summative			
Program	Formative			
	Summative			
Classroom	Formative			
	Summative			

Note: Assessment is generally not applicable to shaded cells.

Worksheet 8   A Rating Scale for Implementing Curriculum and Instruction for Language Education Programs

This rating scale is based on four categories of features that define elements of curriculum and instruction within language education programs illustrated in Figure 3.1.

First, read the following statements and indicate the degree to which you agree or disagree, based on evidence from your program: DK = don't know; 1 = strongly disagree; 2 = disagree; 3 = agree; 4 = strongly agree.

Then, use the information to target areas for strengthening services.

Features of Curriculum and Instruction in Language Education Programs	
Relative Use of Languages	
1. There is a clearly articulated plan for language allocation by grade level for each language group.	DK 1 2 3 4
2. There is a theoretical and practical rationale for the plan.	DK 1 2 3 4
3. The plan outlines language use by content area.	DK 1 2 3 4
4. The plan stipulates the amount of time per day or week for each language by language group.	DK 1 2 3 4
5. The language of assessment mirrors that of instruction.	DK 1 2 3 4
6. Teachers self-monitor and adhere to the plan.	DK 1 2 3 4
Integration of Language and Content	
7. Thematic units of instruction tie language proficiency and academic content standards.	DK 1 2 3 4
8. Language and content objectives frame lesson planning.	DK 1 2 3 4
9. There are ample supports for students (visual, graphic, interactive) for both language and academic development.	DK 1 2 3 4
10. Instruction is differentiated for both language and content.	DK 1 2 3 4
11. Although language and content are integrated for instruction, at times, they are assessed separately.	DK 1 2 3 4

(continued)

Continuity and Duration of Services					
12. The language education program functions within the school's or district's general education program.	DK	1	2	3	4
13. There is a logical and realistic plan for students' progression of language development over multiple years.	DK	1	2	3	4
14. Teachers coordinate services within language education programs.	DK	1	2	3	4
15. There is continuity from year to year in language education services for the students.	DK	1	2	3	4
16. Teachers are involved in sustained professional development to ensure ongoing articulation.	DK	1	2	3	4
17. Documentation of students' language development and academic achievement are maintained from year to year.	DK	1	2	3	4
18. Parents are involved in and informed about the language education program.	DK	1	2	3	4
The Rigor of Teaching and Learning					
19. Teachers jointly plan for assessment, curriculum, and instruction.	DK	1	2	3	4
20. There is thoughtful deliberation in the selection of learning standards.	DK	1	2	3	4
21. Students' educational backgrounds are considered in crafting assessment, curriculum, and instruction.	DK	1	2	3	4
22. The students' linguistic and cultural diversity are used as resources in designing and delivering assessment, curriculum, and instruction.	DK	1	2	3	4
23. Teachers challenge students with accessible, engaging, hands-on learning opportunities.	DK	1	2	3	4
24. Teachers scaffold instruction through interrelated activities and tasks.	DK	1	2	3	4
25. Students are given continuous feedback on their performance.	DK	1	2	3	4

Worksheet 9 Developing Your Assessment Plan: Identifying Formative and Sumative Assessments

First, list specific formative and summative measures that you use to assess student learning and achievement in the areas of (1) cross-cultural competence, (2) second language development, and (3) academic learning in your context. For each measure note if it is administered in L1, L2, or both languages.

Then evaluate the strengths and weaknesses of your assessment plan relative to each learning goal.

Learning Goals, Learning Standards and Learning Benchmarks

	Cross-Cultural Competence	Second Language Development	Academic Learning
Areas of assessment	• Cross-cultural understanding • Intercultural communication • Cross-cultural problem solving and collaboration	• Listening • Speaking • Reading • Writing	• Language Arts • Math • Science • Social Studies
Language(s) of assessment			
Formative assessments			
Summative assessments			

Worksheet 10 Developing Your Assessment Timeline

Based on your assessment plan, develop a timeline to ensure that all assessments are implemented at appropriate points throughout the course of the school year. Keep in mind that you need to balance assessment purposes (formative and summative) so that assessment doesn't interfere with instructional time. Whenever possible, assessment should be integrated with instruction.

	Formative Measures *Assessment for Learning*	Summative Measures *Assessment of Learning*
August/September		
October		
November		
December		
January		
February		
March		
April		
May		
June		

Worksheet 11 Selecting Appropriate Common Assessments to Include in the Pivotal Portfolio

Directions: Use these questions to determine whether the assessments you use are appropriate for the pivotal portfolio.

Name of assessment: Area of assessment:	Yes	No	Why/Why Not?
Is it aligned with best assessment practice?			
Does it give useful feedback to students for learning purposes?			
Does it help teachers make effective, timely classroom instructional decisions?			
Can it be easily integrated into daily instruction?			
Does it yield information about both student growth and achievement?			
Does it produce authentic, performance-based student work samples or artifacts?			

Worksheet 12 Planning Sheet to Select Common Assessments for Dual Language Programs

Directions:

Step1: Select and list one or two common assessments for each type of information, for each group of students, and each area of learning. First list all federal and state tests in appropriate boxes. Then fill in with locally adopted or developed measures, for each language.

Step 2: Review the plan, taking into consideration the types of data that need to be collected and how they may or may not inform instruction and program decisions. Eliminate duplication and invalid and unreliable assessments, as appropriate.

Step 3: Select and list formative assessments that are most easily integrated with daily instruction. Find ways to minimize time spent on testing. Use the BASIC model in Chapter 3 as your reference guide. Consider using other contextual information as well.

Dual Language Assessment—Summative

	Language and Literacy Growth		Academic Achievement	
	Native English Speakers	Native Spanish Speakers	Native English Speakers	Native Spanish Speakers
L1				
L2				

Dual Language Assessment—Formative

	Language and Literacy Growth		Content Learning	
	Native English Speakers	Native Spanish Speakers	Native English Speakers	Native Spanish Speakers
L1				
L2				

Worksheet 13   Creating Spanish as a Second Language Checklists
(Grade Levels K-6)

Directions: The following Spanish-as-a-second-language (SSL) checklists were created by the dual language staff of Schaumburg Community Consolidated School District 54 on April 1, 2005. They are reprinted here with permission. Use and/or adapt these checklists for your dual language program.

Student Name _____

Date(s) assessed _____

Kindergarten SSL Checklist

Oral Performance Indicators	Beginning	Developing	Secure
Produces or repeats isolated words and high-frequency phrases.			
Responds to a greeting/introduction with one word or phrase.			
Uses polite terms of *por favor* and *gracias.*			
Identifies primary colors.			
Identifies family members and friends.			
Sings familiar songs such as the alphabet song.			
Chorally participates in calendar activities (counting, days of the week, weather).			
Reading Performance Indicators	Beginning	Developing	Secure
Listens to a read-aloud and answers basic comprehension questions in English.			
Asks questions to clarify meaning in English regarding text written in Spanish.			
Actively participates in shared and echo reading.			

Writing Performance Indicators	Beginning	Developing	**Secure**
Copies environmental print.			
Attempts to write some familiar words.			
Vocabulary Knowledge Performance Indicators	0–10 words	10–20 words	**20–30 words**
Demonstrates comprehension and usage of new core, targeted vocabulary words.			

First Grade SSL Checklist

Oral Performance Indicators	Beginning	Developing	**Secure**
Initiates, responds to greetings appropriately for time of day.			
Uses familiar phrases and simple sentences in appropriate context.			
Lists vocabulary words according to specific categories.			
Actively participates in routine oral language activities (songs, shared reading, calendar, daily routine).			
Reading Performance Indicators	Beginning	Developing	**Secure**
Recognizes the letters and sounds of the Spanish alphabet.			
Demonstrates interest in Spanish books.			
Reads aloud controlled vocabulary with understanding (colors, numbers, etc.).			
Reads aloud simple picture books and matches text to picture with teacher guidance in order to demonstrate comprehension.			
Actively participates in shared reading and demonstrates comprehension by retelling in English.			

(continued)

Worksheet 13 (*Continued*)

Uses cognates to guess meaning of words.			
Demonstrates comprehension of key vocabulary from a story with prompting.			
Writing Performance Indicators	*Beginning*	*Developing*	**Secure**
Writes short familiar phrases and sentences using sentence starters.			
Spells familiar words correctly in writing activities. (journal, dictation)			
Grammar Usage Performance Indicators	*Beginning*	*Developing*	**Secure**
Uses the present tense of the following verbs in first person singular. (estar, ser, tener, ir, gustar)			
Vocabulary Knowledge Performance Indicators	*0–20 words*	*20–35 words*	**35–50 words**
Demonstrates comprehension and usage of new core, targeted vocabulary words.			

Second Grade SSL Checklist

Oral Performance Indicators	*Beginning*	*Developing*	**Secure**
Answers basic questions and responds appropriately in simple phrases when spoken to in Spanish.			
Makes simple requests to the teacher.			
Actively participates in a variety of oral language activities (songs, shared reading, calendar).			
Reading Performance Indicators	*Beginning*	*Developing*	**Secure**
Reads aloud simple text at first-grade level with understanding and accuracy.			

	Beginning	Developing	Secure
Uses context and cognates to guess meanings of words.			
Demonstrate comprehension by describing a favorite part of a simple story.			
Demonstrates comprehension by completing a story map accurately with characters and setting after reading.			
Follows simple written directions accurately.			
Writing Performance Indicators	*Beginning*	*Developing*	**Secure**
Writes sentences following learned Spanish conventions and spelling patterns.			
Writes a simple paragraph using sentence starters or frames.			
Grammar Usage Performance Indicators	*Beginning*	*Developing*	**Secure**
Uses present tense verbs accurately in simple sentences in speaking and writing (*-ar* verbs in first and third person).			
Uses definite and indefinite articles appropriately in speaking and writing (*el, las, los, las/un, una, unos, unas*).			
Writes with correct use of adjective agreement (gender and number).			
Vocabulary Knowledge Performance Indicators	*0–20 words*	*20–35 words*	**35–50 words**
Demonstrates comprehension and usage of new core, targeted vocabulary words.			

Third Grade SSL Checklist

Oral Performance Indicators	*Beginning*	*Developing*	**Secure**
Initiates conversation and responds in complete sentences when appropriate.			

(continued)

Tells a personal story in complete sentences with teacher's prompt or assistance.			
Makes requests to the teacher and other students.			
Demonstrates willingness to speak Spanish with peers in class.			
Reading Performance Indicators	*Beginning*	*Developing*	**Secure**
Chooses appropriate books for independent reading.			
Reads aloud second grade text with fluency and understanding.			
Demonstrates comprehension by completing a story map with characters, setting, and events.			
Demonstrates comprehension by retelling stories accurately with graphic or text support.			
Demonstrates ability to apply the reading strategies of predicting and making connections.			
Identifies the topic/main idea in an expository paragraph.			
Follows written directions to complete an activity without assistance.			
Writing Performance Indicators	*Beginning*	*Developing*	**Secure**
Writes three paragraphs about family members, friends, activities or school subject.			
Demonstrates use of outside sources in writing when appropriate (dictionaries, word walls, texts).			
Grammar Usage Performance Indicators	*Beginning*	*Developing*	**Secure**
Uses appropriate pronouns to replace nouns in speaking/writing.			

Use the verbs *ser, estar* and *ir* accurately in the present and past tense in speaking and writing (in all persons).			
Uses the present tense construction *ir + infinitive* accurately to express future in speaking and writing (in all persons).			
Edits for correct use of adjective agreement in writing.			
Vocabulary Knowledge Performance Indicators	*0–20 words*	*20–35 words*	**35–50 words**
Demonstrates comprehension and usage of new core, targeted vocabulary words.			

Fourth Grade SSL Checklist

Oral Performance Indicators	Beginning	Developing	Secure
Initiates the discussion of a topic in a social and academic setting.			
Uses vocabulary learned through the content areas correctly.			
Tells a story in simple sentences without a teacher's prompt or assistance.			
Demonstrates willingness to speak Spanish with peers in and out of class.			
Reading Performance Indicators	*Beginning*	*Developing*	**Secure**
Reads a variety of books independently with comprehension.			
Reads aloud third-grade text with fluency and intonation that indicates understanding.			
Demonstrates comprehension of third-grade text through various means.			

(continued)

Demonstrates comprehension by retelling a story independently with accurate and elaborate details.			
Demonstrates ability to apply the reading strategies of predicting, making connections and summarizing.			
Identifies the topic/main idea and important details in an expository text.			
Writing Performance Indicators	*Beginning*	*Developing*	**Secure**
Writes a three-paragraph narrative or expository essay using appropriate transitional words and Spanish conventions.			
Responds to content area questions in complete comprehensible sentences.			
Grammar Usage Performance Indicators	*Beginning*	*Developing*	**Secure**
Uses present, past and future tenses or -*ar,* -*er,* and -*ir* verbs correctly in speaking and writing.			
Uses adverbs correctly in speaking and writing.			
Vocabulary Knowledge Performance Indicators	*0–20 words*	*20–35 words*	**35–50 words**
Demonstrates comprehension and usage of new core, targeted vocabulary words.			

Fifth/Sixth Grade SSL Checklist

Oral Performance Indicators	*Beginning*	*Developing*	**Secure**
Initiates and discusses topics of interest in academic settings.			
Narrates a story and describe with detail.			
Maintains and sustains a conversation with others including questions and complete sentences.			

Demonstrates willingness to speak Spanish with others in and out of class.			
Reading Performance Indicators	*Beginning*	*Developing*	**Secure**
Uses context and cognates to predict specialized, academic word meanings.			
Demonstrates ability to apply reading strategies (predicting, making connections, questioning, summarizing and inferring).			
Demonstrates comprehension of fourth grade text through various means.			
Demonstrates understanding of expository by completing an appropriate graphic organizer.			
Reads/uses a variety of tools to research assigned topic.			
Writing Performance Indicators	*Beginning*	*Developing*	**Secure**
Uses complex sentences in writing.			
Writes essays on a variety of topics with precision and details.			
Uses organizational vocabulary in writing to transition and conclude formal essays.			
Composes a well-organized research report on an assigned academic topic.			
Grammar Usage Performance Indicators	*Beginning*	*Developing*	**Secure**
Uses a full range of grammar structures in speaking and writing. (including imperfect, simple past, and subjunctive).			
Vocabulary Knowledge Performance Indicators	*0–20 words*	*20–35 words*	**35–50 words**
Demonstrates comprehension and usage of new core, targeted vocabulary words.			

Directions: Follow the directions inside each box to design a local assessment reference chart that helps educators in your context guide instructional decision making about your ELLs in the transitional bilingual education programs.

L2 Oral Proficiency	L2 Reading and Writing Proficiency	L2 Academic Functioning Level
Level I Include here cut-off scores, levels of oral proficiency describing beginning level functioning ELLs, based on common formative and summative ESL measures used in your program.	Include here cut-off scores, levels or reading and writing proficiency describing beginning level of literacy functioning of ELLs, based on common formative and summative literacy measures used in your program.	List classroom evidence required to show that ELLs are unable to function independently in a monolingual English setting in most or all academic subjects and need major curricular modification. (e.g., report card, teacher's observation, and student-selected work samples.)
Level II Include here cut-off scores, levels of oral proficiency describing intermediate level functioning of ELLs, based on common formative and summative ESL assessment measures used in your program.	Include here cut-off scores, levels of reading and writing proficiency describing intermediate level of literacy functioning of ELLs, based on common formative and summative literacy assessment measures used in your program.	List required classroom evidence and summative test results to show that ELL is able to function in a monolingual English setting with some tutorial help and modification in major core subjects (e.g., report card, local and state tests, teacher's observation, and student-selected work samples).

Level III Include here cut-off scores, levels of oral proficiency describing high functioning ELLs, based on common formative and summative ESL assessment measures used in your program.	Include here cut-off scores, levels of reading and writing proficiency describing high functioning literacy of ELLs, based on common formative and summative literacy assessment measures used in your program.	List required classroom evidence and summative test results to show that ELL is able to function independently at grade level in a monolingual English setting in most academic classes with minimal support and accommodation (e.g.,: report card , local and sate tests, teacher's observation, and student-selected work samples).
Level III/Transition Include here cut off scores, minimal level of oral proficiency needed to meet program and state criteria for ELLs to exit the program, based on common, formative and summative ESL assessment measures used in your program.	Include here cut-off scores, minimal level of reading and writing proficiency needed to meet program and state criteria for ELLs to exit the program, based on common formative and summative literacy assessment measures used in your program.	List required classroom evidence and minimal summative test scores to show that ELL is able to function independently at grade level and be academically successful in a monolingual English setting, thus is ready to exit from the program.

Worksheet 15   Developing a Cover-sheet for the Student's
Cumulative Record

Directions: The following Student Cumulative Record Form is adapted from the Student Cumulative Record Form created by Schaumburg School District 54, and it is reprinted here with permission. Using this form as a model, develop a cover-sheet for use in a pivotal portfolio for your language education program that reflects your program goals, structure, and assessments.

TBE STUDENT'S CUMULATIVE RECORD

Student: _____   ID#: _____

Birthdate: _____   Entrance Date: _____

Primary Language: _____   Exit Date: _____

Base School: _____   Reason: _____

YEARS IN PROGRAM

Year	Teacher (Content, ESL)	Grade	Attending School	Telephone

A. STANDARDIZED ASSESSMENT

ENGLISH LANGUAGE PROFICIENCY TEST

Date	Oral Language Level and Designation	Reading Scores and Designation	Writing Scores and Designaton	Overall Proficiency Student Designation

SPANISH LANGUAGE PROFICIENCY TEST (if applicable)

Date	Oral Language Level and Designation	Reading Scores and Designation	Writing Scores and Designaton	Overall Proficiency Student Designation

STATE ACADEMIC ACHIEVEMENT TEST
(Administered in grades . . .)

Date	Grade	Test Name	Score and State Designation				
			Reading	Writing	Math	Science	Social Studies

DISTRICT ACADEMIC ACHIEVEMENT TEST (ENGLISH AND SPANISH IF APPLICABLE)
(Administered in grades . . .)

Date	Grade	Test Name	National Percentile Score			Total NP
			Reading NP	Language NP	Math NP	

OTHER STANDARDIZED TESTS

Date	Test Name	Scores	Comment

(continued)

Worksheet 15 (*Continued*)

B. FORMATIVE ASSESSMENT

SPEAKING PROFICIENCY

I. Oral Proficiency   (Samples are collected at least once a year.)

Date	Comprehension	Fluency	Vocabulary	Pronunciation	Grammar	Comments

READING PROFICIENCY

II. Reading Matrix   (Samples are collected at least once a year.)

Date	Engagement	Word Analysis	Comprehension	Language Assessed

WRITING PROFICIENCY

III. Writing Proficiency Matrix   (Samples are collected at least twice a year.)

Date	Focus	Support	Organization	Language Production	Conventions	Language Assessed

INFORMAL READING INVENTORIES (IRIs)

		Score			Reading Level		
Date	Name of Inventory	Word Analysis	Comprehension	Independent	Instructional	Frustration	Language of Test

PLAN FOR TRANSITION

ACADEMIC SUBJECTS IN GEN. ED. CLASSROOMS	PERIOD		GRADE	COMMENTS
	FROM	TO		
MATH				
SCIENCE				
SOCIAL STUDIES				
LANGUAGE ARTS				

Transition period completed on _____.

C. EXIT PROCEDURES*

Consultation with the Director of Program for ELLs or designee was held on _____
The following documents were reviewed:
_____ Most recent report card
_____ General Education Teacher's Recommendation for Transition
_____ Student's pivotal portfolio
_____ Other
Items discussed at this meeting: _____

_____   _____
Bilingual/ESL Teacher   Date

_____   _____
Director, Program for ELLs /Designee   Date

Worksheet 16 Assessing a Second Language Learner's Writing Proficiency

Directions:

1. Look at Lorena García's autobiographical writing in English (from Chapter 5). Use School District 54's rubric for assessing the writing proficiency of second language learners (below), and assess Lorena García's writing. If you were Lorena's teacher, what might you recommend in a conference with Lorena? What instructional strategies might you use?

My Autobiography

What is your life about? My life started in November 13, 1994. I was born in the hospital Metropolitan. The Metropolitan hospital is located in San Antonio, Texas thatís the state I was born in. My favorite colors are green and pink. When I started pre-school is when I learned English. I had to move from Skokie, Chicago to Hoffman Estates. My sister skipped kinder, however I went to kinder and thatís where I met all my friends I know now. My teacher for kinder was Mrs. Mosquera. My first grade and second was Mrs. Medina. My third grade teacher was Mrs. Rosales. My fourth grade teacher was Ms. Garcia and my fifth grades teachers are Mrs. Hernandez and Ms. Beaty. When I entered fifth grade I moved again to Schaumburg. The clubs that I'm in right now are girl scouts, world leaders, band, after school band, and battle of the books. For band I play the clarinet, I would like to learn how to play the guitar. In my life there has been ups, downs, embarrassing, and funny moments. The best day in my life in the year 2006 was when I heard my niece talk to me for the first time on the phone. The worst day was when I heard my uncle Beto died in Mexico. The most embarrassing moment was when I called my grandpa dad. The funniest day would probably be when I tripped my sister and she fell down and almost cried but started to laugh. My life to me has been kind of interesting. Oh, before I forget my family is Juan, my dad, Marisela, my mom, Liliana, my sister, Me, Carla, my sister, Güero, my dog and my niece Analyah my sister Liliana's baby.

Thank You

---

2. Select a piece of writing that one of your second language learners has produced, and assess it using a rubric that is commonly used to assess the writing proficiency of second language learners in your context. If you don't have a rubric to assess the writing proficiency of second language learners in your context, use School District 54's rubric and adapt it as appropriate. Discuss the strengths and needs of the student with your colleague, and brainstorm appropriate instructional strategies.

Writing Proficiency Matrix for Grades 2–8

Student's Name _____ Grade _____ School _____

Writing Type _____ Rated _____ Date _____

Directions: For each of the 5 categories, mark an "X" across the box that best describes the student's performance.

	1	2	3	4	5	6
Focus How the writer introduces and develops a topic, main ideas, and details	No main idea or topic.	Topic is extremely unclear or confusing.	Unclear topic, with some main ideas stated. Ideas are unrelated and not explicitly clear.	Fairly clear topic. Main ideas stated but not developed or elaborated. Irrelevant details. Lacks conclusion or has irrelevant conclusion.	Clear topic. Central idea/purpose is explicitly announced in the opening and maintained. Clear conclusion does not contradict opening.	Very clear topic. Includes topic sentence(s) with all main ideas stated. Relevant and integrated details. Clear and relevant conclusion.
Support How the writer explains and elaborates the main idea	Little to no support of topic. Insufficient writing.	Support attempted but undeveloped. May be inaccurate or irrelevant. Insufficient writing.	Most major elements supported with general statements. Elaborations and explanations not integrated with the topic. No second order elaboration.	Accurate but incomplete support of topic. Some second order elaboration. Not much depth of ideas.	Accurate support of topic. Most main points have second order elaboration. Some depth of ideas.	Specific elaboration with balanced second order support. Accurate and credible details integrated to show support of topic in depth.
Organization How the writer shows a logical flow of ideas and a clear text plan	No text plan or attempt at organization	Lack of organization and logical sequencing	Unclear text plan with some logical, but incomplete sequencing. Limited number of transition words. Inappropriate paragraphing.	Loose text plan with some transition words/phrases used correctly. Some appropriate paragraphing.	Clear text plan with logical sequencing and development. Adequate transition phrases. Appropriate paragraphing. Minor digressions may exist.	Very clear text plan with fully developed, logical ideas that are complex and interrelated. No digressions.

(continued)

Language Production How the writer uses vocabulary and sentence structure	Some writing attempted. May use word lists. Words from native language may be present.	Meaning obscured by imprecise / limited vocabulary.	Fragmented / simple sentences. Nonspecific vocabulary that generalizes meaning.	Some expanded sentences, with little variety in sentence structure. Adequate vocabulary, with appropriate use of subject-specific language.	Most sentences clearly written with some variety in sentence length and structure. Accurate use of subject-specific language. Appropriate use of writing type / genre.	Clearly written, complete sentences, demonstrating variety of sentence length and structure. Creative use of vocabulary. Exhibits skillful use of writing type/ genre.
Conventions How the writer uses standardized forms of target language	Few to no conventions present.	Major convention errors make meaning incomprehensible.	Some convention errors that cause confusion in meaning.	Most words spelled correctly. Punctuation and capitalization are mostly correct.	Some minor errors in conventions.	There are no second language learner errors in conventions.

Worksheet 17 Using the BASIC Model for Decision Making: Examining Assessment Data

What data do you collect and how do you use it? Complete the following survey. Use the scale (from 1–3) in the last column to rate how you use different types of data.

Types of Assessment Data in L1 and L2	Purpose for Assessment	Decisions	Level of Decision-making	Data Collected	The extent that these data are used to inform decision making 1 = Not at all; 2 = Somewhat; 3 = Fully
Standardized measures (e.g., language proficiency tests; academic achievement tests in L2 and L1)	**Summative: Assessment of Learning** • Meet accountability requirements • Place and reclassify ELLs • Improve program services	• Student and subgroup progress and attainment of standards • Eligibility and extent of support services	State District Program Classroom	_____ L1 academic achievement _____ L2 academic achievement _____ L1 language proficiency _____ L2 language proficiency _____ Cross-cultural competence	1　2　3 1　2　3 1　2　3 1　2　3 1　2　3
Standard measures (e.g., district writing prompts and rubrics; observation with common checklists; commonly-made performance based assessments)	**Summative and Formative Assessment** • Monitor student growth and achievement • Inform instruction • Guide program and professional development • Determine program impact	• Reconfiguration of language allocation • Curriculum impact and adjustment • Regrouping of students • Effectiveness of unit or lesson • Refinement of this unit or lesson	State District Program Classroom	_____ L1 academic learning _____ L2 academic learning _____ L1 language development _____ L2 language development _____ Cross-cultural competence	1　2　3 1　2　3 1　2　3 1　2　3 1　2　3

(continued)

Worksheet 17   *(Continued)*

Idiosyncratic measures (e.g., surveys, anecdotal notes, student self-assessment)	**Formative: Assessment for Learning** • Determine extent of language support • Document individual behaviors • Regulate and monitor learning	• Grouping of students • Differentiation of instruction • Diagnosis of student strengths and areas for improvement • Grading • Effectiveness of unit or lesson • Refinement of unit or lesson	Classroom Program	_____ L1 academic learning	1	2	3
				_____ L2 academic learning	1	2	3
				_____ L1 language development	1	2	3
				_____ L2 language development	1	2	3
				_____ Cross-cultural competence	1	2	3

Worksheet 18 Developing an Action Plan for Using Assessment Data for Authentic Accountability

Directions: Use the information from Worksheet 17 to formulate a plan for building authentic accountability within your language education program.

1. What do you consider the strengths of the accountability system currently in place for your language education program?

2. Which areas related to data do you need to strengthen?

   • Identification of data sources

   • Data collection

   • Data analysis and interpretation

   • Use of data in decision making

3. How would you devise an action plan to enhance program evaluation within an authentic accountability system? Consider using the elements identified in the following table to outline the important first steps.

	Goal I.	Goal II.	Goal III.
Action(s)			
Resources needed			
Timeline			
Persons involved			

4. How might sustained professional development for teachers and administrators move the plan forward? The time table for the action plan is a good starting place for identifying professional development activities associated with each goal or action.

Glossary

Academic achievement   Students' knowledge and skills learned through the curricular content areas.

Academic content standards   Descriptions of benchmarks of student achievement in the core subject areas.

Academic language   The language skills needed to process and communicate knowledge and skills related to content.

Academic language proficiency   The processing and use of language, including vocabulary in social and academic settings, multiple meanings, register, pragmatics, and sociocultural nuances as well as the quantity and quality of discourse, that help define English language learners' position on the second language acquisition continuum.

Alignment   The degree of correspondence between two entities, such as the extent of match between standards and assessment or between two assessments.

Assessment   The systematic planning, collecting, analyzing, and reporting of student data from a variety of sources over multiple points in time.

Assessment frameworks   Ways of conceptualizing how to gather, display, and use contextual information and student assessment data for educational decision making.

Authentic assessment and accountability   Examination of data systematically collected in educational programs determined by consensus of constituents involved in the decision-making process.

Balanced assessment   The use of multiple and varied measures with input on a formative and summative basis that yield qualitative and quantitative results.

BASIC model   An acronym for "A Balanced Assessment and Accountability System, Inclusive and Comprehensive", a descriptive representation of the use of data in schools and language education programs by teachers and administrators for teaching, learning, and decision making that represents multiple perspectives and provides a rich portrait of students as learners.

Bilingual pivotal portfolio   The cumulative collection of common formative and summative assessment information, exemplified by student original work samples designed to illustrate individual student's progress and achievement in language proficiency, academic achievement, and cross-cultural competence from year to year, during their participation in language education programs.

Common measures   *See* **standard measures**.

Contextual Information   Background information on students and their prior educational experiences which help frame the interpretation of data.

Criterion-referenced measures   A form of assessment or testing based on established criteria, such as standards, rather than ranking based on the performance of students

Cross-cultural competence   A goal of language education programs whereby students are able to comfortably interact and negotiate in various cultural settings and norms.

Cross-sectional data   The comparison of the same type of information on different groups of students from year to year, such as examining the achievement of 3rd graders.

Developmental bilingual education   A form of language education with the goals of building bilingual proficiencies and grade level achievment for students while they gain cross-cultural competence. Foreign language immersion and dual language programs are examples of developmental bilingual programs.

Dual language education   A form of developmental bilingual education that serves English language learners from a common language background, alongside proficient English speakers, with the goals of full development in L1 and L2 oral language proficiency, literacy, and grade-level achievement for both groups of students while gaining cross-cultural competence.

English as a second language (ESL)   A form of language education that serves English language learners from multiple language backgrounds with the goal of full development in L2 (English).

English language learners (ELLs) Students from linguistically and culturally diverse backgrounds who qualify for language support services to reach parity with their proficient English peers.

English language proficiency standards Descriptions of the social and academic language necessary for English language learners to succeed in school as agreed upon at the national (i.e., TESOL), consortium (e.g., WIDA), or state level.

Evaluation The systematic planning, collecting, analyzing, and reporting of data from a variety of sources to determine the effectiveness of educational programs.

Evaluation frameworks Ways of conceptualizing how to gather, display, and use data for judging the effectiveness of educational programs.

External accountability The imposition of data collection, such as the use of a statewide test, from outside a classroom or district, used to make educational decisions.

Foreign language education A type of language education program in which students are exposed to languages and cultures (other than English), generally not part of their backgrounds, with the goal of developing oral language and literacy.

Formative assessment The collection, analysis, and reporting of information on a regular basis that informs students about their progress and learning based on immediate feedback.

Heritage language speakers Proficient English speakers from linguistically and culturally diverse backgrounds who also speak or understand a language other than English.

High-stakes tests Large-scale, summative instruments that tend to influence policy making and whose results have potential consequences for students, teachers, schools, or school districts.

Idiosyncratic measures The planning, collecting, analyzing, and reporting of student data that are unique to individual teachers and their classrooms.

Informal reading inventory A performance-based, formative assessment of students' reading whose results provide an inventory of students' abilities in major aspects of reading, including vocabulary knowledge, listening comprehension, silent reading comprehension, and fluency.

Internal accountability A system of assessment and evaluation in which multiple sources of data are used for monitoring student progress in reaching locally determined goals and making improvements to programs of instruction based on local needs.

L1 A person's first, native, or home language.

L2 A person's second or acquired language (generally English, for English language learners).

Large-scale assessment The use of standard conditions across multiple classrooms (e.g., grade levels, programs, schools, districts) in the collection, analysis, and reporting of student data.

Language proficiency A person's overall competence in processing and using language across the language domains of listening, speaking, reading, and writing.

Level(s) of language proficiency A description of the developmental progression of second language acquisition that has been arbitrarily divided along a continuum.

Longitudinal data The collection of the same information under the same conditions on the same group of students over time.

Native English speakers Students whose primary language background is English.

Normal curve equivalents (NCEs) A statistic descriptive of results from a standardized, norm-referenced test in which the bell curve is divided into 99 equal segments or intervals.

Percentile A statistic descriptive of results from a standardized test determined from a mean and standard deviation of a normal distribution of scores that represents non-equal interval data along the bell curve.

Performance assessment Original student work and performance that are interpreted with scoring guides or rubrics

Proficient English learners Former English language learners who have transitioned from language support services.

Qualitative data Descriptive information about student performance or language education programs.

Quantitative data Analytic information, usually presented numerically, about student performance or language education programs.

Rubrics A uniform set of criteria presented in the form of a scoring guide or scale used to interpret student work on a consistent basis.

Self-assessment Students' monitoring and analysis of their work in which they reflect on their strategies, products, and processes of learning

Sheltered instruction An approach within language education programs that serves English language learners from multiple language backgrounds with the goal of development of academic language in L2 (English) through content and applies to SSL in Spanish to English speakers.

Social language proficiency The language required in understanding, processing, and communicating thoughts and ideas in daily interaction and situations.

Standard measures Assessment that adheres to identical conditions for collection, analysis, and the reporting of student data across multiple classrooms.

Standardized measures Generally, norm-referenced tests in which results indicate ranking of students in relation to those in the norming population.

Student-led conferences Meetings between teachers, student. and parents that are led by students rather than teachers. At the typical conference, students review their goals, provide evidence of whether they have met learning targets, reflect on their learning, and, with the guide of the teacher and parents, set new goals.

Summative assessment The use of standard or standardized measures during a specified time frame, such as on an annual basis, that offers summary information on student performance or program effectiveness.

Transitional bilingual education (TBE) (early exit) A form of transitional bilingual education that serves English language learners from a common language background with the goals of full development in L2 (English), at the sacrifice of their L1, with expectations for grade-level achievement and assimilation into L2.

Transitional bilingual education (TBE) (late exit) A form of transitional bilingual education that serves ELLs and provides them with a gradual transition into the all English environment based on L2 proficiency and academic performance.

Two-way immersion (TWI) *See* **Dual language education**

Validity The extent to which assessment measures and data generated from them are appropriate for and support the decisions made about students and educational programs; the match between a test and its stated purpose.

References

Afflerbach, P. (2005). National Reading Council policy brief: High-stakes testing and reading assessment. *Journal of Literacy Research 37*(2), 151–162.

Ainsworth, L., & Viegut, D. (2006). *Common formative assessments: How to connect standards-based instruction and assessment.* Thousand Oaks, CA: Corwin Press.

American Council on the Teaching of Foreign Languages. (1985). *Revised ACTFL proficiency guidelines.* Hastings-on-Hudson, NY: Author.

Arter, J. (2006a). *Auditing classroom assessments for quality.* Paper presented at the 18th Annual Consortium for Educational Change Summer Institute, Oak Brook, IL.

Arter, J. (2006b). *Designing instructionally powerful rubrics.* Paper presented at the 18th Annual Consortium for Educational Change Summer Institute, Oak Brook, IL.

Arter, J., & Chappuis, J. (2006). *Creating and recognizing quality rubrics.* Portland, OR: Educational Testing Service.

Assessing Comprehension and Communication in English State to State for English Language Learners (ACCESS for ELLs®). (2006). Madison, WI: State of Wisconsin, Wisconsin Center for Education Research.

Black, P., Harrison, C., Lee, C., Marshall, B., & Williams, D. (2004). Working inside the black box: Assessment for learning in the classroom. *Phi Delta Kappan 86*(1), 8–14.

Breiner-Sanders, K., Lowe, P., Jr., Miles, J., & Swender, E. (1999). ACTFL proficiency guidelines–speaking. Revised 1999. *Foreign Language Annals 33*(1). Washington, DC: Center for Applied Linguistics.

Center for Applied Linguistics. (2004). *Rating scale for CAL Oral Proficiency Exam* (COPE). Washington, DC: Author.

Center for Applied Linguistics (1996). *Student Oral Proficiency Assessment* (SOPA). Washington D.C.: Author.

Chappuis, S. (2004). Leading assessment for learning: Using classroom assessment in school improvement. *Texas Association of School Administrators Professional Journal-INSIGHT, 18*(3), 18–22.

Chappuis, J. (2006). *Seven strategies for assessment for learning.* Paper presented at the 18th Annual Consortium for Educational Change Summer Institute, Oak Brook, IL.

Chappuis, S., Stiggins, S., Arter, J., & Chappuis, J. (2003). *Assessment for learning: An assessment guide for school leaders.* Portland, OR: Assessment Training Institute.

Christian, D. (2006). What kinds of programs are available for English language learners? In E. Hamayan & R. Freeman (Eds.), *English language learners at school: A guide for administrators* (pp. 81–82). Philadelphia: Caslon.

Cloud, N., Genesee, F., & Hamayan, E. (2000). *Dual language instruction: A handbook for enriched education.* Boston: Heinle & Heinle.

Collier, V. P., & Thomas, W. P. (2004). The astounding effectiveness of dual language education for all. *NABE Journal of Research and Practice, 2*(1), 1–20. http://njrp.tamu.edu/2004.htm.

Crawford, J. (2006). What does a valid and reliable accountability system for English language learners need to include? In E. Hamayan & R. Freeman (Eds.), *English language learners at school: A guide for administrators* (pp. 6–10). Philadelphia, PA: Caslon.

Darling-Hammond, L., Ancess, J., & Falk, B. (1995). *Authentic assessment in action: Studies of school and students at work.* New York: Teachers College Press.

Darling-Hammond, L., Ancess, J., & Falk, B. (2005). *Authentic assessment in action: Studies of schools and students at work.* New York: Teachers College Press.

DuFour, R., DuFour, R., Eaker, R., & Karhanek, G. (2004). *Whatever it takes: How professional learning communities respond when kids don't learn.* Bloomington, IN: Solution Tree.

Echevarria, J., Vogt, M.E., & Short, D. (2004). *Making content comprehensible to English language learners: The SIOP model.* Boston: Allyn & Bacon.

Flynt, E. S., & Cooter, R.B. Jr. (1998) *Reading inventory for the classroom.* Des Moines, IA: Merrill Prentice Hall.

Fortune, T., & Arabbo, M. A. (2006). *Attending to immersion language proficiency assessment at the program level.* Paper presented at the Dual Language Pre-Conference Institute, NABE 2006, Phoenix, AZ.

Freeman, Y. S., Freeman, D. E., & Mecuri, S. P. (2005). *Dual language essentials for teachers and administrators.* Portsmouth, NH: Heinemann.

Genesee, F. (1985). Second language learning through immersion: A review of U.S. programs. *Review of Educational Research 55,* 541–561.

Genesee, F., Lindholm-Leary, K., Saunders, B. & Christian, D. (2006). *Educating English Language Learners: A Synthesis of Research Evidence.* New York: Cambridge University Press.

Goodrich, H. (1996). Understanding rubrics, *Educational Leadership,* 54 (4), 14–17.

Gottlieb, M. (1999). Assessing ESOL adolescents: Balancing accessibility to learn with accountability for learning. In C. J. Faltis & P. Wolfe (Eds.), *So much to say: Teenagers, bilingualism and ESL at the secondary school* (pp. 176–201). New York: Teachers College Press.

Gottlieb, M. (2003). Large-scale assessment of English language learners: Addressing accountability in K-12 settings. *TESOL Professional Papers no. 6.* Alexandria, VA: Teachers of English to Speakers of Other Languages.

Gottlieb, M. (2006). *Assessing English language learners: Bridges from language proficiency to academic achievement.* Thousand Oaks, CA: Corwin Press.

Gottlieb, M. (2007). *ELL assessment kit.* (2007). Austin, TX: Rigby.

Gottlieb, M., & Nguyen, N. D. (2005). Developmental bilingual education in the real world: Using longitudinal data to enhance dual language program development. In Cohen, J., McAlister, K., Rolstad, K., & MacSwan, J. (Eds.). *ISB4: Proceedings of the 4th International Symposium on Bilingualism* (pp. 935–947). Somerville, MA: Cascadilla Press.

Gottlieb, M., Carnuccio, L., Ernst-Slavit, G., & Katz, A. (2006). *PreK–12 English language proficiency standards.* Alexandria, VA: Teachers of English to Speakers of Other Languages.

Gregory, G. H., & Kuzmich, L. (2004). *Data driven differentiation in the standards-based classroom.* Thousand Oaks, CA: Corwin Press.

Guskey, T. R. (2003). How classroom assessments improve learning, *Educational Leadership, 60 (5), 6–11.*

Hilliard, J. (2005). *Dual language teacher training curriculum.* Des Plaines: Illinois Resource Center.

Howard, E., & Sugarman, J. (2001). *Two-way immersion programs: Features and statistics* (EDO-FL-01–01). Washington, DC: Center for Applied Linguistics.

Idea Proficiency Test (IPT). (2001). Brea, CA: Ballard and Tighe.

Illinois Measure of Annual Growth in English (IMAGE). (1996). Springfield, IL: State of Illinois.

Illinois Standards Achievement Test (ISAT). (1999). Springfield, IL: State of Illinois.

Johns, J. (1997). *Basic reading inventory: Pre- primer through grade twelve and early literacy assessments.* Dubuque, IA: Kendall/Hunt.

Kibler, J. & Nguyen, D. (2002). *Dual U- Dual language teacher training curriculum: Cross-cultural learning module.* Des Plaines, IL: Illinois Resource Center.

Lachat, M. A. (2004). *Standards-based instruction and assessment for English language learners.* Thousand Oaks, CA: Corwin Press.

Lambert, W. E., & Tucker, G. R. (1972). *The bilingual education of children: The St. Lambert experiment.* Rowley, MA: Newbury House.

Leslie, L., & Caldwell, J. (2001). *Qualitative reading inventory,* 3rd edition. New York: Longman.

Lindholm-Leary, K. J. (2001). *Dual language education*. Clevedon, UK: Multilingual Matters, Ltd.

Lindholm-Leary, K. (2006). What are the most effective kinds of programs for English Language Learners? In Hamayan, E. & Freeman, R. (Eds.), *English Language Learners at School: A Guide for Administrators* (pp. 84–85). Philadelphia: Caslon Publishing.

Miramontes, O. F., Nadeau, A., & Commins, N. L. (1997). *Restructuring schools for linguistic diversity: Linking decision making to effective programs*. New York: Teachers College Press.

National Clearinghouse for English Language Acquisition. (2005). The growing number of Limited English Proficient students 1993/94–2003/04. Retrieved July 8, 2006, from http://www.ncela.gwu.edu/policy/states/reports/statedata/2003LEP/GrowingLEP_0304_Dec05.pdf

Nichols, S., Glass, G., & Berliner, D. (2006). High-stakes Testing and Student Achievement: Does Accountability Pressure Increase Sudent Learning? *Education Policy Analysis Archives*, 14(1).

Northwest Evaluation Association. (2003). Des Cartes Learning Continuum. Portland, OR: Author.

Northwest Evaluation Association. (2006), *Measures of Academic Progress*. Lake Oswego, OR: Author.

O'Malley, J. M., & Valdez Pierce, L. (1996). *Authentic assessment for English language learners: Practical approaches for teachers*. New York: Addison-Wesley.

Popham, W. J. (2003). *Test better, teach better: The instructional role of assessment*. Alexandria, VA: Association for Supervision and Curriculum Development.

Shephard, L. A. (April 1989). Why we need better assessments. *Educational Leadership 46*, 4–9.

Shephard, L. A. (2000). *The role of classroom assessment in teaching and learning*. Los Angeles: National Center for Research on Evaluation, Standards, and Student Testing.

Snow, M. A., & Brinton, D. M. (Eds.). (1997). *The content-based classroom: Perspectives on integrating language and content*. White Plains, NY: Addison-Wesley.

Stiggins, R. (2006a). *It's time for an assessment revolution*. Keynote speech at the 18th Annual Consortium for Educational Change Summer Institute, Oak Brook, IL.

Stiggins, R. (2006b). *Policy and program leadership for excellence in assessment*. Keynote speech at the 18th Annual Consortium for Educational Change Summer Institute, Oak Brook, IL.

Stiggins, R. J. (2002). Assessment crisis: The absence of assessment FOR learning. *Phi Delta Kappan*, 83(10), 758–765.

Stiggins, R., Arter, J., Chappuis, J., & Chappuis, S. (2004). *Classroom assess-

ment for student learning: Doing it right—Using it well. Portland, OR: Educational Testing Service.

Stiggins, R., & Chappuis, C. (2006). What a difference a word makes: Assessment FOR rather than assessment OF learning helps students succeed. *National Staff Development 27*(1), 10–14.

SUPERA. (1997). Monterey, CA: CTB McGraw Hill.

TerraNova. (1997). Monterey, CA: CTB McGraw Hill.

Thomas, W. P., & Collier, V. (1997). *School effectiveness for language minority students.* Washington, D.C.: George Washington University, National Clearinghouse for Bilingual Education.

Thomas, W. P., & Collier, V. P. (2002). *A national study of school effectiveness for language minority students' long-term academic achievement.* University of California, Berkeley: Center for Research on Education, Diversity & Excellence.

Tierney, R., Carter, M., & Desai, L. (1991). *Portfolio assessment in the reading-writing classroom.* Norwood, MA: Christopher Gordon Publishers.

U.S. Department of Education. (2001). *The No Child Left Behind Act of 2001.* P.L. 107–110. Washington, DC: Author.

Vygotsky, L. (1978). *Mind in society: The development of higher psychological processes.* Cambridge, MA: Harvard University Press.

Wagner, S. (2001). *Crossing classroom borders: Pathways to the mainstream through teacher collaboration.* Dissertation, University of Illinois at Chicago, College of Education.

Wiggins, G. P. (1993). *Assessing student achievement: Exploring the purpose and limits of testing.* San Francisco: Jossey-Bass.

World-Class Instructional Design and Assessment ACCESS Placement Test (W-APT) (2006). Madison, WI: State of Wisconsin, Wisconsin Center for Education Research.

World-Class Instructional Design and Assessment (WIDA) (2005). Spanish language arts standards. Madison, WI: State of Wisconsin Center for Education Research.

Wormeli, R. (2006). *Fair isn't always equal: Assessing and grading in the differentiated classroom.* Portland, ME: Stenhouse.

Index

Note: Page numbers followed by f refer to figures; page numbers followed by t refer to tables.